D0215036

Aquinas and the Jews

John Y. B. Hood

University of Pennsylvania Press
Philadelphia

Printed in the United States of America

Library of Congress Cataloging-in-Publication Data
Hood, John Y. B., 1962–
Aquinas and the Jews / John Y.B. Hood.
p. cm. — (Middle Ages series)
Includes bibliographical references and index.
ISBN 0-8122-3305-0. — ISBN 0-8122-1523-0 (pbk.)
1. Judaism—Relations—Christianity. 2. Christianity and other religions—Judaism. 3. Christianity and antisemitism—History. 4. Thomas, Aquinas, Saint, 1225?–1274—Views on Judaism. 5. Judaism (Christian theology)—History of doctrines—Middle Ages, 600–1500. I. Title. II. Series.
BM535.H63 1995
261.2′6′092—dc20 95-5296
CIP

For Debra

Contents

Introduction

In 1965, the Catholic Church revised its traditional teaching on the Jews and their place in history. In their "Declaration on the Relation of the Church to Non-Christian Religions" (*Nostra Aetate*) the bishops of the Second Vatican Council rejected the idea that all Jews were guilty of the Crucifixion of Jesus, declared persecution of Jews to be immoral, and informed catechists and other religious educators that "the Jews should not be spoken of as rejected or accursed."[1] These statements were brief and undramatic; the section on Jews in *Nostra Aetate* is only two pages long. The bishops did not overtly acknowledge that they were altering traditional doctrine, nor did they strike a penitential note. When the decree was promulgated, however, it was immediately recognized that the Church had repudiated more than fifteen hundred years of theory and practice.

Prior to Vatican II, no theologian was more closely identified with traditional Catholic teaching than Saint Thomas Aquinas (1224–1274). A controversial figure during his lifetime, Aquinas was accepted as the official philosopher of the Dominican Order within a generation of his death, and by the end of the Middle Ages he had eclipsed such rivals as Duns Scotus to become the Church's most influential theologian. At the Council of Trent his *Summa Theologiae* lay on the altar next to the Bible. Over the next three centuries, Aquinas's popularity waxed and waned, and the Church did not follow his teaching on every issue (the doctrine of the Immaculate Conception, which was promulgated by Pope Pius IX in 1854, despite the fact that Thomas had denied it, is a case in point), but his theological method and many of his substantive ideas remained regnant. His star shone even more brightly after 1879, when Pope Leo XIII promulgated the encyclical *Aeterni Patris*, which lavished praise on Aquinas and called for a greater emphasis on the Angelic Doctor's teaching. Catholic philosophers, theologians, and historians enthusiastically responded to Leo's challenge and made the period from 1880 to 1960 a golden age of Thomism. Aquinas became virtually the Church's official philosopher and theologian, and countless books, articles, and dissertations were published on every aspect of his thought.

Significantly, very few of these works dealt with Aquinas's attitude toward Jews. In the aftermath of the Dreyfus affair, two French pamphlets were published on Aquinas and the Jews, one accusing him of being an "antisemite," the other defending him from the charge.[2] In 1935 another brief, apologetic treatment appeared.[3] Even in the years since World War II, when a debate has raged over the allegedly Christian roots of modern anti-semitism, only a handful of articles on Aquinas's attitude toward Jews have been published.[4] This is the first book-length treatment of the topic.

Since Aquinas wrote widely on both Judaism and the status of Jews in a Christian society, this neglect cannot be explained by a lack of source material. Rather, its causes must be sought in the attitudes and interests of Aquinas scholars. Most of these scholars have been either self-proclaimed "Thomists" who have looked to Aquinas as a source of philosophical and religious truth, or else historians of medieval thought. It is not difficult to surmise why Thomists have largely ignored Aquinas's teachings on the Jews. These scholars are primarily interested in aspects of Thomas's work which have continuing relevance. Since Aquinas's ideas about Jews seem outdated and intolerant in a modern context, there has been little incentive for Thomists to explore this area of his thought. In addition, most Thomists are conservative Catholics who no doubt are disinclined to deal with issues that could make Aquinas—and, by implication, the Church—appear in a bad light. For them, perhaps, some things are better left unsaid.

The case of medieval historians is more puzzling, but it is of a piece with a broader lack of interest in Jews and Jewish-Christian relations. Medievalists traditionally have been content to leave such topics to specialists in Jewish studies, who, for their part, are neither trained for nor especially interested in studying medieval Christian thought. Over the past decade, however, a handful of scholars have begun to examine the nexus between Christian theology and the status of Jews in medieval society. Much of the impetus for this work has been provided by Jeremy Cohen's *The Friars and the Jews*.[5] In this book Cohen sought to supplement traditional explanations of the persecution of western European Jews in the thirteenth century, persecutions which culminated in the expulsion of Jews from England in 1290 and from France in 1306. Prior to his work, most analyses had focused on four factors: politics, economic developments, popular hostility toward Jews, and the role of the institutional Church, particularly the papacy. Cohen argued that an additional factor should be considered: the ideas and activities of the mendicant religious orders. His position is uncompromising: "Dominican and Franciscan friars . . . engaged in a concerted effort to undermine the religious freedom and physical security of the medieval Jewish community."[6] In support of this thesis, Cohen examined the views of Nicholas Donin, Pablo Christiani, and other friars who developed and aggressively pursued schemes to convert Jews to Christianity. He concluded that thirteenth- and fourteenth-century mendicants brought about a revolution in theological attitudes toward Jews which helped pave the way for persecution and expulsion.

Cohen's position has been widely criticized. Robert Chazan, for instance, argues that Cohen overestimated the impact which the discovery of the Talmud and other Jewish religious texts had on Christians' perception of Judaism.[7] A more obvious problem is that Cohen selected his evidence rather carefully; his book focuses on relatively marginal figures such as Raymond Marti while completely ignoring influential mendicants like Albertus Magnus and Hugh of St. Cher.

This same selectivity mars Cohen's treatment of Thomas Aquinas. Aquinas is not central to his argument, but Cohen does quote a few passages from the *Summa Theologiae* and generally implies that Thomas was part of a theological movement that saw twelfth-century tolerance of Jews give way to fourteenth-century persecution. This implication is false. Aquinas was not part of a radical new trend; on the contrary, his attitude toward Judaism and the Jews was essentially conservative. Thomas's primary goal in this area was to clarify and systematize traditional theological and canonistic teaching on the Jews rather than to break new ground. His teaching was innovative largely in the direction of tolerance rather than persecution. Finally, to the extent Aquinas was aware of new, anti-Jewish trends in theology or in missionary activity, he was either skeptical or actively opposed to them.

This is not to say that his work can tell us nothing about why Christians persecuted Jews in the thirteenth and fourteenth centuries. On the contrary, though his direct causal role was minimal, Aquinas's thought is deeply relevant for understanding these developments. Cohen's basic insight, that theology played a central role in the development of oppressive social policies, is correct and important. What is misleading is his claim that a theological revolution preceded that development. No such revolution was necessary, nor did one occur. The mainstream Christian theological view of Jews and their place in history was substantially the same in 1400 as it had been in 1200. The persecutions and expulsions of the intervening two hundred years did not reflect fundamental theological changes; rather, they proved that the medieval attitude toward Jews was ambiguous enough to justify relatively oppressive as well as relatively tolerant social policies. All that was required was a shift in emphasis.

For medieval theologians like Thomas Aquinas, Jewish history was divided into two periods: B.C. and A.D., the "time under the Law" and the "time of grace," the Old Testament and the Christian era. The hinge joining them was Christ, or, more specifically, his Crucifixion. In both these periods, as well as in the pivotal event of Jesus' death, theology demanded the Jews play a dual role. No medieval theologian doubted that the Jews were the chosen people of God who had received the Law, or that their history was a preparation for the coming of Christ. At the same time, however, theologians explained the Jews' rejection of Jesus by tracing a steady spiritual decline from the faith of Abraham and Moses to the malice and hypocrisy of the Pharisees. Analogously, several New Testament passages forced Christians to admit that the first-century Jews who called for Jesus' execution did not know he was the Messiah and the Son of God, yet patristic theology and canon law made it equally clear that all Jews were in some sense guilty of murdering Christ. Finally, medieval Christians believed Jews would eventually accept Christ and be saved, but they also saw them as dangerous infidels who had been rejected and punished by God.

This dualistic view of Jews and Jewish history, rooted in the New Testament and the teachings of the Church Fathers, was universally accepted by the Christian theologians of the Middle Ages. Its various elements were repeated in sermons, Bible commentaries, and theological treatises until it became an unquestioned and perhaps unquestionable part of the medieval world-view. Aquinas played no role in developing this tradition, nor, *pace* Cohen, did he work to alter it in any significant way. His importance in the history of Christian attitudes toward Jews lies elsewhere. First, as a scholastic theologian with a talent for making cogent distinctions, Aquinas presented the received view of Judaism and the Jews in an unusually coherent form. The great Dominican expressed clearly and completely what others stated piecemeal or merely felt. As such, his writings are a convenient locus and touchstone of the received view. Second, as a theologian whose influence in western Christendom is rivaled only by Augustine, Aquinas has served as a major conduit of the traditional Christian view of Jews for some seven hundred years. Finally, in his quest for system and clarity, Aquinas occasionally came face to face with the dualities of the received view. That is, he made an effort to explain how it was possible for Jews to be at the same time chosen *and* rejected, ignorant *and* malicious Christ-killers, damned *and* destined for salvation. His answers to these questions are often unconvincing, and at times he seems determined to avoid precisely those points that seem to us most important. But at least he asks the questions. More than any other writer of the period, Aquinas lays bare the latent contradictions in the medieval Church's teaching on Jews.

This is so despite the fact that Aquinas did not write a topical treatise on the Jews. On this issue, as on so many others, his key ideas are scattered throughout a number of texts. Even his so-called *De Regimine Iudaeorum* ("On the Governing of Jews") only deals with a handful of specific political and social questions. There are a few places where Thomas discusses Judaism at length, such as the long section on the Mosaic Law in the *Summa Theologiae*, but much of what he has to say about the Jews and their role in history is diffused throughout various works, especially his Bible commentaries. Thus, the task of reconstructing his thought demands a synthetic approach. Fortunately, this presents few problems. Aquinas's thought was not marked by dramatic change or evolution; rather, he developed most of his distinctive ideas early in his career and defended them consistently to the end of his life. Hence in juxtaposing texts which Aquinas wrote at different times there is little risk of doing violence to his thought. This danger is further reduced by the fact that the key works for analyzing his ideas on the Jews—the *Summa*, the *De Regimine Iudaeorum*, and the commentaries on Romans, Matthew, and John—were all written during the last decade of his life.

This material will be organized historically. That is, Aquinas's views on Jews will be examined in a series of chapters that focus on what he believed were the central events in Jewish history: the revelation of the Mosaic Law, the Crucifixion, and the refusal of Jews in the Christian era to accept Jesus as the Christ. Some may object to this approach on the grounds that it is non-Thomistic. Certainly it must be granted that Aquinas was not primarily a historical thinker. In his *Summa Theologiae*, for instance, he rejected sacred history as an organizing principle for systematic theology, opting instead for a more schematic plan. But the Jews are a special case. Here Aquinas's ideas *were* rooted in a particular conception of sacred history. For Aquinas, the Jews are important precisely because of their role in history, and his conception of the Jewish people was structured by specific historical events. Although much of what he says about the Jews is located in works that are organized topically or schematically, this historical backdrop is always present. For this reason I will trace what Aquinas said about Jewish history from Abraham to the thirteenth century in an effort to answer three specific questions: What was Aquinas's attitude toward Jews and Judaism? What were its social and theological sources? What role did his teaching play in the persecution of European Jews?

Before turning to these questions, however, we must first examine their contexts. Like all writers, Aquinas was shaped by literary traditions and specific historical circumstances, and these must be considered in interpreting his words. In the case of his views on Judaism and the Jews, the relevant contexts are three: the history of Christian theology, thirteenth-century Christian-Jewish relations, and the development of medieval canon law on Jews.

1. The Theological Tradition

The break with Judaism was the definitive, oedipal event in the history of Christianity. With their decision to turn their backs on the faith of their fathers and abandon the effort to convert their fellow Israelites, the leaders of the nascent Church redirected their energies toward the infinitely more ambitious—yet, paradoxically, more practical—goal of spreading the Gospel to the ends of the earth. It was a brilliant move, one which inaugurated a breathtaking series of events that saw Christianity grow from a minor Jewish sect into the most influential ideology and set of institutions in world history. Yet the break was not clean. Rather, it was accompanied by hard words and harder feelings and a vague promise that at some point the battle would be rejoined. And so it was. While there were long periods of latency throughout the medieval and early modern periods, Christian frustration at the Jews' refusal to accept Jesus as the Messiah resurfaced time and again, especially at moments of internal crisis. Then the old arguments were dusted off, philippics were composed, and there was a spasm of missionary activity which, after early signs of promise, ended in failure. Finally the movement either collapsed in exhaustion, or—more frequently—erupted in acts of violence.

The ultimate source of this recurrent preoccupation with Jews was, of course, Jesus himself. Not only was Christianity's putative Messiah a Jew; more important, Judaism provided the context for everything he said and did. His messianic claims, his scriptural quotations and allusions, his attacks on the Pharisees and temple priests, and his sacrificial death are all intelligible only in terms of Jewish history and scripture. Nor is it possible to accept Jesus as Messiah without also believing in the Mosaic covenant, the Davidic monarchy, and the divine inspiration of the Hebrew scriptures. In a very real sense, anyone who wishes to become a Christian must first become a Jew.

But if Christianity has historically required its converts to accept the scripture, history, and theology of Judaism, it has also demanded that they utterly eschew its ritual practices. This ambiguous attitude—approbation of Judaism's creed, condemnation of its cult—arose from the decision of the Church's leaders in the second century to excommunicate Christians who continued to observe the ritual precepts of the Law. It was then that the phrase "Jewish Christian" became a contradiction in terms. This development was not inevitable. The words and actions of Jesus were ambiguous on the issue of the Law, so much so that the earliest Christians continued to observe at least some of its ritual precepts and to frequent the Jerusalem Temple. Furthermore, the apostolic decision to free Christians from the regulations of the Mosaic Law was originally tactical rather than doctrinal: circumcision and the various dietary precepts were hindering missionary work among non-Jews. Only later did the early Fathers begin to argue that continued observance of the Mosaic precepts involved an implicit denial of Christ. Jesus, they declared, had not merely fulfilled biblical Judaism; he had established a new religion which had supplanted Judaism as the one true faith, and his followers constituted a new tribe which had replaced Israel as the chosen people of God. Jesus' nuanced position had been transformed into a stark choice: Christian or Jew, Christ or the Law.

Patristic theologians claimed this supersession theory followed logically from elements in the Bible itself, particularly certain passages from the Gospels and Paul. But Jews and other critics of Christianity were quick to point out that it flew in the face of a number of texts from the Hebrew scriptures and the New Testament. For instance, they argued that the notion that the Law has been invalidated contradicts passages such as Leviticus 16.29 which clearly state that the Law was a perpetual covenant. They also emphasized Matthew 5.17–19, where Jesus declares in no uncertain terms that he has *not* come to abolish or even alter the Law. Finally, they noted the tension between the supersession theory and passages in Acts which depict the Apostles attending Temple services, observing at least some of the Mosaic dietary regulations, and performing various other ritual acts prescribed by the Law—all *after* the death, resurrection, and ascension of Jesus.

For most modern commentators, these passages pose little difficulty. Since they view the Bible as a complex, heterogeneous work based on a variety of written and oral traditions rather than as seamless revelation, they are not troubled by textual discrepancies. But for patristic writers, who believed the Bible was an internally consistent whole, revealed by God in oracular fashion, it was imperative that every verse of the sacred text be reconciled with the supersession theory. Over a period of several centuries, the Fathers devoted enormous intellectual energy to the task of explaining away apparent inconsistencies between scripture and the Church's doctrine.

Medieval theologians continued this work, both in their monasteries and—after 1200—in the emerging *studia* and universities of western Europe. Their task was complicated by the fact that, in addition to believing in an inerrant Bible, they were also committed to patristic and ecclesiastical authority. Acceptance of sacred tradition meant that in order to achieve a coherent position on the relation of Christianity to Judaism (as well as on other theological issues), scholars not only had to show that the Bible was internally consistent; they also had to "prove" that it supported the teachings of patristic writers and the medieval Church. These additional strata of texts placed heavy demands on the learning and ingenuity of medieval exegetes. But at the same time it clarified their task by giving them a sense of where they were headed. Difficult or ambiguous passages were less perilous when a commentator could simply invoke the Church's teaching to support his interpretation. For many modern readers, of course, it is precisely this attitude toward authority that renders medieval Bible scholarship unsatisfying and even repulsive. The spectacle of some of the greatest minds in European history devoting their lives to the systematic misinterpretation of ancient texts is truly one of the wonders of intellectual history.

But medieval exegesis was not purely a matter of finding textual support for foregone conclusions. The Church had not spoken on all matters, and even where doctrines had been established there was often room for a variety of positions within the bounds of orthodoxy. Certainly this was true of the relationship between Christianity and Judaism. Naturally, there were certain givens—the supersession theory, the belief that the Old Testament was rife with prefigurative "types" of Christ and the Church, and the notion that the Jews *in toto* were guilty for killing Jesus—but there was also considerable room for originality, both in reconciling the various elements of the tradition and in resolving secondary and marginal issues.

Thomas Aquinas was eminently suited for such a project. As a scholastic theologian, he believed his vocation was to bring the categories of Aristotelian logic and metaphysics to bear on the Bible, the writings of the Church Fathers, and the pronouncements of the medieval church in order to produce a unitary synthesis of Christian wisdom. The relation of Judaism to Christianity was only one of many issues Aquinas dealt with in pursuit of this synthesis, but the myriad links between the two religions made it a topic he returned to again and again. As in much of Thomas's work, there is a dual strain to his thought. On the one hand, we see him engaged in the mundane task of reconciling medieval doctrine with what the Bible and the Fathers say about Judaism. But simultaneously, in a more creative mode, he uses the authoritative texts for guidance and inspiration in developing his own positions on questions the Church had not definitively resolved.

Because Thomas was utterly dependent on literary sources—the New Testament and the writings of the Church Fathers—in developing his views on Judaism, it is imperative that we examine these sources at some length. Without question, the New Testament was the most important influence. As a theology professor in Paris and elsewhere, Thomas taught courses on it for more than a decade, and he also wrote commentaries on two of the Gospels (Matthew and John) and on all of Paul's letters. Though he read the Bible in light of Catholic dogma and through the filter of the standard medieval commentaries, especially the *Glossa ordinaria*, it was the sacred text itself which did most to shape his thought.

Much of the New Testament is devoted to Christianity's relation to Judaism, a fact that reflects the early Christian community's obsession with this issue. Despite some initial conversions, most first-century Jews continued to reject the *kerygma*, the fundamental Christian proclamation that Jesus of Nazareth was the Messiah who had died and was risen. This rejection, together with the Jewish claim that belief in Jesus was heretical, eventually forced Christians to reexamine the relation of their faith to Judaism.

The period from A.D. 50 to 100 was the formative era in the history of Christianity. At the beginning of this half-century, Christianity was a small Jewish sect nourished by an oral tradition recounting the words and actions of Jesus. By the year 100, Christianity was an explosive missionary religion with growing numbers of adherents, most of them Gentile, throughout the Mediterranean world. Furthermore, all the writings that would eventually be included in the New Testament canon were composed during this period. Finally, and not least important, the parameters of a definitive, orthodox position on the relation of Christianity to Judaism were coming into focus. The position that would prevail in the early Church, it was increasingly clear, would not be grounded in the ambiguous statements of Jesus recorded in the Gospels. Rather, it would be based on the writings of Paul.[1]

Four themes dominate Paul's discussion of the relation of Christianity to Judaism.[2] The first is that the Jews are the chosen people, the recipients of the divine promises and the divine law. Abraham was chosen by God to be the founder of a people consecrated to God. To this people the land of Palestine was promised. In due time God rescued them from slavery, and, through Moses, gave them his Law at Sinai. For Paul, the divine origin and intrinsic righteousness of the Law is beyond question. "The Law is holy, and the commandment is holy, just and good" (Rm. 7.12). The Law given to Moses teaches true morality, forbids idolatry, and places the people of Israel in a unique and special relation to God.

A second Pauline theme is that the Law, for all its virtues, is limited and imperfect. The Mosaic commandments teach what is right, but they cannot provide the ability to do it. In itself the Law is holy, but human beings, weak and inclined to sin as they are, experience the Law more as a reproach then a help. It provides an understanding of what is right, but this only serves to increase sin, for when people do wrong under the Law they do so in full knowledge that their actions are sinful. Thus the Law cannot save; in fact, it condemns. "As many as are of the works of the Law are under a curse" (Gal. 3.10a). Yet its effects are not wholly negative, for while the Mosaic Law cannot justify human beings in the sight of God, it does serve as a pedagogue: it provides a basic knowledge of God and morality, and it convicts humans of sin and thus teaches them that they need forgiveness and grace. In this way the Law prepares the way for a fuller revelation of God's nature and will.

For Paul, Judaism has been superseded by the revelation of Christ. This is the third major theme of his teaching. Justification is now to be had not by keeping the commandments of the Law, but through faith in the redemptive death of Jesus Christ. According to Paul, the death of Jesus brought an end to the legal dispensation, destroyed the distinction between Jew and Gentile, and brought into existence a new economy of salvation. "In Christ Jesus, you that used to be so far apart from us have been brought near in the blood of Christ. For he is the peace between us, and has made [Jew and Gentile] into one and broken down the barrier, destroying in his own flesh the hostility and making void the law of commandments contained in the decrees, that he might make the two in himself into one new man, making peace" (Eph. 2.13–14). Faith in Jesus is not merely an alternative or addition to the Law; it has replaced it. To continue to believe that the Law is salvific is to reject Christ, who is now the sole means of salvation. "For the end of the Law is Christ, to the justification to all who believe" (Rm. 10.4). And because they have refused to accept Christ, the Jews have "fallen." Now, as the prophets foretold, God has taken to himself a new people.

Finally, Paul declares that the Jews' lapse is only temporary. "The Jews are enemies with regard to the Gospel . . . but as regard to election they are beloved for the sake of their ancestors. For the gifts and call of God are without repentence" (Rm. 11.28–29). In the past the people of Israel had been sent into exile as punishment for their unfaithfulness, only to return to the Holy Land when they had repented; in the same way they will regain God's favor when they come to accept Christ. Furthermore, Paul indicates the conversion of the Jews will mark the consummation of the divine plan. In the last days, all shall be united in Christ, with every division and distinction destroyed, and with this the *parousia*, the full coming of the kingdom of God, will arrive.

Paul's analysis did not lack rivals. Ebionites and other Jewish-Christian groups in Palestine continued to observe the precepts of the Mosaic Law, claiming that in doing so they were fulfilling Jesus' true intentions. On the other side, Manicheans, Gnostics, and Marcionites argued that the Mosaic Law was intrinsically irrational and immoral, and that the God of the Hebrew scriptures was not the Father of Jesus Christ but was actually Satan or an evil demiurge. But each of these groups was successfully marginalized in the second century with the gradual coalescence of a body of authoritative Christian writings which included Paul's letters. Thereafter all orthodox Christian speculation on the relation between Christianity and Judaism was carried on within Pauline parameters.

Though Paul's writings were the dominant influence on the way the Church Fathers thought about Judaism, the Gospels and the Book of Acts were important as well. The nature of their impact, however, was rather different. Patristic writers found the Gospels disturbingly ambivalent on the doctrinal relationship between Christianity and Judaism. The Sermon on the Mount (Mt. 5–7) shows Jesus transforming the Law by shifting the focus from external action to intentionality, and in three of the Gospels Jesus claims he has come to "fulfill" the Law of Moses. But the nature of this transformation and fulfillment is not entirely clear. A literal reading of Matthew 5.17–19 ("Not a dot, not an iota . . .") certainly supports the contention that Jesus intended his followers to continue to observe the ritual commandments of the Law, and if Jesus and his disciples occasionally violated the Sabbath with impunity (Mt. 9.14–17; Lk. 6.1–5; Mk. 2.18–22), they also visited the Temple (Jn. 18.20) and observed the Passover feast (Mt. 26.17–19; Mk. 14.12–16; Lk. 22.7–13). Nor could the Church Fathers look to the Book of Acts to clarify matters. Acts records the fact that the apostles visited the Temple to pray (Acts 3.1), and also notes that Paul himself had Timothy circumcised (Acts 16.3) and kept a Nazarite vow (Acts 21.20–26).

According to Acts, Peter, the head of the Church at Jerusalem, received a revelation that all foods were ritually pure, which indicated Christians did need not to keep the dietary precepts of the Law. Nevertheless, when the apostles met to decide whether Gentile Christians had to keep the legal precepts, the result was a compromise in which Gentiles were absolved from most ritual commandments but were obliged to keep a few, and nothing was said regarding the obligations and liberties of Jewish Christians regarding the Law (Acts 15.1–29). In sum, the relationship between Christianity and Judaism depicted in Acts and the Gospels was ambiguous at best, as various groups of judaizing Christians eagerly pointed out. To resolve this dilemma, patristic theologians relied on Paul to provide them with their understanding of the doctrinal position of Christianity vis-à-vis Judaism, then used various ad hoc strategies to reconcile Pauline doctrine with problematic texts in the Gospels and Acts.

At the same time, the narrative books of the New Testament provided patristic authors with something Paul did not: a detailed picture of Jewish society at the time of Christ. Paul had much to say about the Law, but very little about the Jews as such. He saw them as sincere but in error ("I give testimony that they have zeal for God, but it is not according to knowledge" [Rm. 10.2]) and his attitude toward his former coreligionists was one of concern and regret, leavened by hope. He was grieved by the Jews' rejection of Jesus, and at one point even said he would willingly be cut off from Christ if he could thereby effect their salvation (Rm. 9.2–3), but he was confident they would ultimately be restored to their position of preeminence. Beyond this, however, Paul was silent, and he offered little guidance on the burning question of why the Jews had rejected, and continued to reject, the claims of Jesus to be the Messiah. For this, patristic theologians had to look to the Gospels.

All four Gospels divide the Jews into two basic groups: the common people on the one hand, and their leaders—the elders, scribes, priests, and Pharisees—on the other. The evangelists portray the Jewish masses as generally well intentioned, if weak and misguided. Jesus is compassionate toward them: he heals the sick, feeds the multitudes, miraculously provides wine for a wedding, and preaches to them in popular fashion, employing many parables and metaphors. In return the people respond to Jesus with great interest. They turn out en masse to hear him preach, hail him as a prophet, and wonder if he might be the promised Messiah. But their interest and devotion is short-lived. In time most of his followers abandon him, and in the end a Jerusalem mob demands his execution.

By contrast, the evangelists are uniformly critical of the leaders of first-century Judaism. In the Gospels, the scribes, priests, elders, and Pharisees are malevolent and hypocritical. Sticklers for fine points of the Law, they ignore its humanitarian spirit in their zeal for minutiae that have little to do with true righteousness. These leaders are consistently portrayed as elitist and ostentatious: they pray loudly and publicly, wear fine robes, sit at the front of the synagogue, and are careful that everyone notice when they fast or give alms. Jealous of their prestige and power, they obstinately refuse to believe in Jesus' divine mission in spite of the astonishing miracles he performs. Instead, they claim his powers are demonic in origin, they belittle his ancestry and learning, and they repeatedly ask him sophistical questions about the Law, hoping he will trip up and be publicly humiliated. Throughout Jesus' public ministry, the Pharisees' hostility increases, and eventually they conspire to have him arrested and executed. To accomplish this they spread rumors to incite the masses against Jesus, then bribe Judas Iscariot to betray Jesus to the Temple guards.

In each of the four Gospels, the climactic crucifixion episode begins with a monkey trial before the Jewish authorities, who accuse Jesus of blasphemy then escort him to the Roman authorities to secure his execution. In a final act of cynical manipulation, they incite the crowd to call for Jesus' crucifixion and question Pontius Pilate's loyalty to Rome when he appears reluctant to give the order. Pilate washes his hands to show that he is free of personal responsibility for the execution; meanwhile, the Jewish crowd, inspired by its leaders, takes the responsibility on itself: "Let his blood be upon us and upon our children" (Mt. 27.25).

There was a crucial difference between the Gospels' vivid—if one-sided—portrait of first-century Jewish society and Paul's theological critique of Judaism. The writings of Paul, as the Church Fathers saw it, were a conduit of eternal theological truth. His declaration that Christ had abrogated the Law, for instance, was not subject to subsequent change or revision. It was an immutable article of faith. But the Gospels' depiction of Palestinian Jewry was another matter. These were historical truths, not theological dogmas. As such, the Church Fathers had to accept them as accurate for the Jews of Jesus' time, but they were not obliged to regard them as valid descriptions of all Jews everywhere. Yet this is precisely what they did.

In retrospect, it is easy to see why. In the Gospels, it is the malevolence of the Jews that explains their rejection of Jesus. For Christian writers in the early centuries of the common era, faced with a sizable population of

Jews who continued to resist the call to accept Jesus, this model provided a convenient excuse for the Church's missionary failures. It had strong psychological appeal as well. The Jews' refusal to convert to Christianity was potentially scandalous. How could the Jews reject Jesus, Christians asked themselves, if the Hebrew scriptures testified he was the Messiah? This was a dangerous question. Absent a ready answer, Christians might have begun to wonder if they were proclaiming the Gospel effectively, or if their lives bore witness to the truth of their faith. Placing the blame on the "blindness" and "hardheartedness" of Jews provided a readymade way to avoid such doubts. In this way the Gospels' portrait of first-century Jewish society was hypostatized into a rigid cultural stereotype: the willful, stubborn Jew. The only significant patristic development of this stereotype was negative: In time, Christian writers began ascribing to all Jews the negative traits the Gospels had attributed to the Pharisees alone.

While the New Testament provided the normative framework for subsequent discussion of the Jews and their role in salvation history, it left at least four major issues unresolved. One involved the nature of the Mosaic Law and the religious and moral character of Old Testament Jews. Although Paul had indicated that the Law was good but imperfect, there was much to be done to specify what this meant, and the New Testament writers had done little toward constructing a synoptic view of Jewish history. A second set of questions arose from patristic efforts to clarify the notion that the Jews had been "rejected" by God because they did not believe in Christ. Third, various Christians speculated about God's purposes in allowing the Jews to continue to exist. Finally, the coexistence of Christians and Jews in the Mediterranean world generated endless questions about social and religious interaction.

Several factors influenced the way patristic writers approached these issues, including their theories of biblical exegesis, their personal contacts—if any—with Jews, whether or not a writer was confronted with "judaizing" Christians, and sheer personality. History played an important role as well. All patristic writers saw the hand of providence at work in the destruction of the Jewish Temple in A.D. 70 and in the expulsion of the Jews from Jerusalem in 135. The Church Fathers believed these events had fulfilled New Testament prophecies and vindicated their claim that God had rejected the Jews. Subsequent developments reinforced this perception: the gradual christianization of the Roman Empire, the failed attempt to rebuild the Temple during the reign of Julian the Apostate (361–63), and the decline of Jewish proselytizing activity. Reflecting on these events, patristic writers were convinced that the triumphs of the Cross and the disasters that had befallen the Jews proved that Christians were the new chosen people, the "*verus* Israel."[3]

For Aquinas and other theologians of the Latin West, Saint Augustine (354–430) was by far the most important of the Church Fathers. Just as Augustine's views on free will, predestination, and Trinitarian dogma remained paradigmatic for a thousand years, so too his ideas on Judaism and the Jews dominated the medieval debate. This was so despite the fact that Judaism and the Jews are not major themes in Augustine's voluminous writings. Primarily a topical writer, the bulk of Augustine's work consists of sermons, letters, and polemical treatises defending Catholic doctrine against the four great heresies of the age (Manicheanism, Donatism, Pelageanism, and Arianism). Though Jews were present in Italy and North Africa—the regions with which Augustine was most familiar—it seems they did not attempt to convert Christians, nor were Italian or African Christians especially attracted to Jewish ceremony and ritual; had a significant number of Christians converted to Judaism or engaged in "judaizing" practices, Augustine undoubtedly would have felt compelled to confront Judaism more often. Because he did not see Judaism as a major threat, and because he was more a polemicist than a systematic theologian, there were relatively few contexts in which Augustine dealt with Judaism and its relation to Christianity.

Nevertheless, Augustine's status in the Middle Ages was such that his comments on any topic, however sparse, were inevitably important. An example of this phenomenon was Augustine's theory that God might have implanted "seminal natures" (*rationes seminales*), or latent principles of change, into all things at the beginning of creation. Though this notion was merely a bit of offhand speculation designed to resolve a problem in biblical interpretation, medieval scientists argued over its merits for several centuries.[4] Similarly, while the passages in Augustine's writings which are relevant to Judaism constitute only a tiny fraction of his total output, his unparalleled authority lent them tremendous influence.

Augustine discussed the role of the Jews in salvation history in *The City of God*, and his *Contra Faustus* is largely a defense of the Christian interpretation of the Mosaic Law. Various references to Jews are also scattered throughout his biblical commentaries, most notably in his *Enarrationes super Psalmos*. Finally, he devoted a brief sermon to the issue of Judaism and the Jews, the so-called *Tractatus contra Iudaeos*.[5] Little of what he wrote in these texts was entirely original, but with characteristic lucidity he consolidated scattered elements of patristic thought, providing medieval theologians with a coherent view of the Mosaic Law and the role of Jews in the Christian dispensation. His views were subsequently incorporated wholesale into the Latin theological tradition; Augustinian themes appear regularly in medieval Bible commentaries, theological treatises, and papal decrees. Just as the New Testament provided the parameters within which subsequent Christian thought on Judaism and the Jews developed, so Augustine was the founder of the specific approach which became dominant in the medieval West.

The overarching theme in these texts is the claim that the Mosaic Law and all of Jewish history were significant only as a prelude to Christianity. According to Augustine, God designed the Law's rituals to symbolize Christ and the Christian sacraments. Augustine grants that the moral commandments of the Mosaic Law are universal truths, and he also notes that many of the ritual precepts were intrinsically reasonable because they helped inculcate reverence for God. But, he argues, not all the ceremonial commandments can be explained on rational grounds. Augustine claims, for instance, that the commandment not to boil a goat in its mother's milk had no meaning except as a typological symbol. And even when he allows that a particular ceremonial commandment was partly designed to meet the historical needs of the Jews, Augustine still insists that its prefigurative sense was more important. Furthermore, he claims some Old Testament Jews knew this. According to him, people like Moses and Aaron realized that the Law's precepts were mere shadows of the reality that was to come. Most Jews, to be sure, did not achieve this level of understanding, but a chosen elite did, and Christians were the successors of this elite. In this sense, he argued, Christianity was not a new religion at all, but merely the full blossoming of an ancient faith. Enlightened Jews of the Old Testament period believed in the Messiah who was to come; Christians believed in Christ whose incarnation was now a past and present reality.

Having shown that the faith of Christians was one with that of ancient Israel, Augustine went on to explain the apostolic decision to free Christians from the precepts of the Law. His defense contained two elements. First, he stressed the relative inadequacy of Mosaic religion. Relying heavily on the New Testament's *Letter to the Hebrews*, he argued that animal sacrifice was crude and ineffective and had been replaced by the one true sacrifice of Christ. Similarly, he claimed that other Mosaic rituals were religiously unsatisfying because they concentrated on the external, were difficult and burdensome, and were incapable of conferring grace.

By contrast, the Christian sacraments imparted internal, sanctifying grace. Second, Augustine made the audacious claim that the Hebrew scriptures themselves had indicated that the Mosaic Law would be abrogated with the coming of the Messiah. In his view, the Mosaic commandments were valid for a given time only, and that time had now passed. Rather than violating the Law, Christians were actually acting in accord with its true intentions.

From this, Augustine argued, it follows that it is actually the Jews who have abandoned the faith of their fathers. Moses and the other heroes of the Old Testament understood that the Law was merely a prelude to Christ, but latter-day Jews have foolishly absolutized it. Thus Christians are the true heirs of Moses, while the Jews are apostates. This paradox highlights the basic character flaws of the Jews: spiritual blindness, disobedience, and "carnality," by which Augustine meant the tendency to focus on the literal sense of scripture to the exclusion of its symbolic and spiritual meaning. Augustine believed these flaws had deep roots in the Old Testament period. He acknowledged that the Jews in the time before Christ were morally and intellectually superior to pagans, but he placed much more emphasis on their shortcomings than on their virtues. Drawing on prophetic denunciations of the Jews—without regard for context or hyperbole—Augustine concluded that the Jews were chronically disobedient and idolatrous. He believed the period after the establishment of the second Temple was an especially dark age in Jewish history, an era of spiritual decline that reached its nadir at the time of Christ, when the Jews did the work of Satan by rejecting and crucifying their own Messiah.[6]

Thus far, Augustine was at one with the mainstream of the patristic tradition. His prefigurative reading of the Old Testament was derivative and pedestrian, as was the way he transformed prophetic rhetoric and Jesus' denunciations of the Pharisees into a rigid stereotype—the stubborn, sinful Jew—then used that stereotype to explain away the Church's missionary failures. On such issues, Augustine's writings on the Jews are important only because they were the primary vehicle that carried these ideas to medieval theologians such as Aquinas.

But Augustine was not content merely to explain why the Jews had not accepted Christ. For him, history was the stage on which God's providential design was acted out. God was the consummate artist, and he permitted no unintegrated facts into the drama of salvation history; every detail must enhance the beauty of the whole. Even apparent flaws actually contributed to the greater good. The Jews' unbelief, their willful decision—as Augustine saw it—to deprive themselves of the salvation offered by Christ, was no doubt evil in itself, but even this contributed somehow to the fulfillment of God's plan. Taking a hint from Romans 10, he argued, with astonishing boldness, that the unbelief of Jews actually promoted the spread of the Christian message.

Augustine claimed that Jews aided Christian missionaries in two ways. First, their status as homeless exiles, with their Temple destroyed, testified to God's rejection of the Jews and adoption of the Christians as the new chosen people, the *verus Israel*. Second—and here Augustine was most original—the continued existence of the Jews furnished positive evidence of the truth of Christianity. If the Jews did not exist, he argued, then pagans would accuse Christians of inventing the Old Testament prophecies that point to Jesus. But the Jews precluded such attacks; they were living proof of the antiquity of the Hebrew scriptures.[7] In this way the continued existence of the Jews went hand in hand with the spread of the Christian gospel. Augustine supported this theoretical argument with an empirical claim: Where you find Christians, he said, you invariably find Jews as well. In the Augustinian scheme of sacred history, the Jews serve as unwitting John the Baptists, preparing the way for the Good News.

It would be difficult to overstate how ingenious this theory was, or how important a role it would play in Jewish-Christian relations during the Middle Ages. Not only did Augustine's argument mitigate the scandal caused by the Jews' resistance to the Gospel, it also provided a foundation for tolerating Jews within a Christian society. From an Augustinian perspective, it was imperative that the Jews continue to exist, since the fortunes of Christianity were closely linked to those of Judaism. Furthermore, Augustine's notion that the Jews had a positive role in the divine plan, together with Paul's claim that the Jews would convert in the last days, inhibited Christian efforts to convert them. It is true that for six hundred years after Augustine's death there was no political or ecclesiastical structure in the West sophisticated enough to impose systematic pressure on the Jews, nor were more than a handful of princes or clerics interested in making such an effort. But, beginning in the eleventh century, with the development of the crusading ideal and the concentration of power in the hands of the papacy and centralized nation-states, there was suddenly both the will and the means to impose such pressure. From 1050 on, Church and state hunted down heretics, Moslems, and pagans with ever-increasing ferocity. It was largely the Augustinian view of Judaism and the Jews, integrated into theology and canon law, that shielded the Jews of western Europe from the full force of Christendom's coercive powers. Had it not been for Augustine's theory of the positive role of their unbelief—and

Paul's prophecy of their future conversion—the Jews of medieval Europe would have been offered the same choice given to heretics: Convert or die.

Before turning our attention to other patristic writers who helped shape medieval attitudes toward Jews, we should note three further aspects of Augustine's thought. First, though he used prophetic invective to denounce contemporary Jews and constantly stressed their blindness and carnality, Augustine's anti-Jewish polemic was generally stylized and devoid of malice. Certainly he never attacked them with the ferocity he displayed in condemning the Manicheans and other heretics. In fact, in the *Tractatus contra Iudaeos*, he urged Christians to treat Jews with kindness and compassion. Salvation was an unmerited gift from God, he stressed, and Christians should not gloat over the Jews' fall.[8] Two factors may help explain this relatively humane attitude: Augustine was not writing in the midst of an active confrontation with Jews or judaizers;[9] and his conviction that the Jews' unbelief was part of the divine plan led him to deemphasize their personal culpability. But whatever its source, his moderation undoubtedly had a restraining influence on later Christian thinkers.

Second, though Augustine knew little Hebrew and had no regular contact with Jewish scholars, he did occasionally refer to Jewish interpretations of scripture, and in principle he was not opposed to conferring with Jewish scholars or using their works as aids in interpreting the Bible. This attitude was nothing new; Origen, for example, had made extensive use of rabbinic sources in his biblical commentaries. But the example of Augustine undoubtedly helped assure medieval scholars that it was legitimate to consult Jewish exegetical works.

Augustine's final contribution to medieval thought on Jews—his position on the question of Jewish guilt—had a very different effect on Christian attitudes. Patristic authors without exception agreed that the destruction of the Temple and the exile of the Jews were divine punishments, but they differed over the precise nature of their crime. Some, like Tertullian and Origen, said that the sin was simply their failure to accept Jesus as the Messiah. Others, such as Gregory the Great, argued that it was the Jews' persecution of the Apostles. Augustine's analysis was more pointed. The Jews, he said, were being punished for killing Christ. In his view, it was irrelevant that the first-century Jews who had called for Jesus' crucifixion were long gone, for he believed that contemporary Jews were equally guilty. "Occidistis Christum in parentibus vestris," Augustine declared in the *Tractatus contra Iudaeos*—"In your ancestors, you killed Christ." As he saw it, the Jews' refusal to accept Christianity constituted de facto acquiescence to Jesus' execution. This theory of Jewish guilt, which eventually became dominant in the Latin West, would have a long and tragic history. Unlike the charge that Jews were guilty of unbelief or of persecuting the apostles, the notion that Jews were deicides was uniquely capable of exciting anger and hatred. Augustine's theory specified and personalized Jewish guilt; it accused Jews of the most brutal imaginable treatment of Jesus, the object of the deepest Christian love and devotion. Augustine did not believe that Jewish guilt gave Christians the right to abuse Jews—the entire thrust of his ideas on the role of Jews in history militated against such a conclusion—nor was he the only Church Father to charge the Jews with deicide, but he played a significant role in adding the tag "Christ-killer" to the long list of negative attributes that formed the popular image of the Jew in the Middle Ages.

Even so, the totality of Augustine's writings had a meliorating influence on medieval Christian-Jewish relations. Despite occasionally vilifying them, Augustine developed the most important argument for tolerating Jews known to the Middle Ages. He also urged they be treated kindly and warned against Christian triumphalism. By contrast, the legacy of his great contemporary, Saint Jerome (349–420), was more ambivalent. Among the Latin Fathers, Jerome's influence on the medieval mind ranks behind only that of Augustine. His translation of the Bible (the "Vulgate" edition) was the version used by most medieval scholars, and his erudite commentaries on Scripture were widely studied, both in their original form and via the copious extracts included in the *Glossa ordinaria*. Though, like Augustine, Jerome accepted the three central axioms of patristic thought on Judaism and the Jews—a prefigurative interpretation of the Old Testament, the theory that Christians had replaced Jews as the chosen people, and the belief that Jews were being punished by God—in other ways his views differed from Augustine's both in tone and substance. Several factors helped shape Jerome's attitude toward Jews, but the most important were his long residence in Palestine (where Jews defended their faith vigorously and where judaizing tendencies among Christians were strong), his interest in Hebrew, and his passionate, irritable personality, which often drove him to rhetorical excess.

Jerome settled in Palestine in 381, primarily in order to study Hebrew. His goal was to master the language so he could produce an accurate Latin translation of the Old Testament. During the ten-year period he was at work on this project, Jerome was in constant contact with Jews, studying under several rabbinic tutors and also meeting with learned Jews in more informal settings. Jerome was an avid pupil, and he respected the rabbis' knowledge of the language, though he sometimes complained that they charged him too much. His masters taught Jerome more than just Hebrew grammar and syntax, however; he was also influenced by their methods of biblical interpretation. According to Marcel Simon, Jerome was "nourished on [the] Jewish traditions he . . . gleaned from the rabbis, who were his masters in exegesis as well as in the Hebrew tongue."[10] These discussions—which, Jerome claimed, the rabbis usually initiated—sometimes degenerated into acrimonious disputes over the meaning of the Hebrew text, with Jerome defending Christological interpretations while the rabbis attacked his position. Such contests honed his polemical skills and, more important, introduced him to the methods of rabbinic exegesis. In many respects Jerome's Old Testament commentaries were a continuation of these verbal debates; his commentary on Psalms, for instance, was specifically motivated by the desire to refute Jewish interpretations.

This context of interaction and competition produced Jerome's complex attitude toward Judaism and Jews. On the one hand, it was he who, more than any other Latin Father, displayed an open appreciation for the original Hebrew version of the Old Testament—the "Hebrew truth" as he called it—as well as a willingness to take into account the views of Jewish exegetes.[11] This rabbinic influence is revealed most clearly in the way Jerome prefaced his typically patristic "spiritual" exegesis of the Old Testament with a real effort to ground his interpretations in the literal meaning of the text. Eight hundred years later, when Andrew of St. Victor set out to expound the Old Testament *ad litteram*, he acknowledged he was following in the footsteps of Jerome, and like his master he saw consultation with Jewish exegetes as an integral part of his project.[12] Augustine had also given a patristic imprimatur to medieval scholars who looked to Jews for help in uncovering the literal meaning of the Old Testament, but it was Jerome who was their true guide along this path.

If Jerome encouraged intellectual contact with Jews, however, he also penned some of the patristic era's most vicious anti-Jewish passages. Jerome never shrank from abusing his enemies, and Jews bore the brunt of some of his most blistering invective.[13] In his view the most fitting symbol for the Jews was Judas, the betrayer of Christ, for like Judas they were malicious, blind, and ungrateful. Jerome accused the Jews of almost every imaginable vice, but avarice, drunkenness, gluttony, and licentiousness were his favorites. Unlike Augustine, Jerome saw little if any positive role for Jews in the plan of salvation; perhaps his experience of Judaism as a living, potent rival made it harder for him to be sanguine about the "witness" Jews gave to the truth of Christianity. In his view, the Jews had alienated themselves from God by their rejection of Christ, and by attempting to lure Christians away from the true faith they acted as agents of Satan. Their continued existence was an affront to God, and their attempts to worship him were blasphemous. In a typical image, Jerome compared the prayers and hymns offered up by Jews to the "grunting of a pig and the bellowing of an ass."[14]

Saint John Chrysostom (344–407) was a near contemporary of both Augustine and Jerome, and along with Gregory of Nyssa, Gregory Nazianzus, and Basil of Caesaria, he was one of the four great Fathers of the Greek Church. Yet it was only in the thirteenth century, when a number of his writings, notably his homilies on the Gospels, were translated into Latin, that he became an important figure for Western theology. In the 1260s, Chrysostom's writings enjoyed something of a vogue in Paris's theological circles. Thomas Aquinas was especially smitten with him; his biographers relate that he once claimed he would rather have a copy of Chrysostom's homilies on Matthew than own all of Paris.[15] Thomas's wish was eventually granted, and he borrowed heavily from this work in composing his own commentary on the Gospel.

Chrysostom's passionate hatred of Jews has long been notorious.[16] His *Discourses Against Judaizing Christians* are the most famous anti-Jewish works in all of patristic literature. In this series of sermons, the "golden-tongued" Chrysostom castigated the Jews with all his rhetorical skill, accusing them of utter moral depravity and even intimating at one point that they should be killed.[17] Because the *Discourses* were not translated into Latin until the fifteenth century, Aquinas and other medieval theologians were not acquainted with this work, the purest distillation of the Greek Father's animus. But hatred of Jews also permeated Chrysostom's exegetical treatises. Unlike Augustine (though like Jerome) Chrysostom saw no positive role for Jews in the Christian dispensation beyond the fact that their degradation proved that God had taken to himself a new people. Otherwise his substantive position was similar to Augustine's; he too believed the Church was the *verus Israel*, that the Law was primarily prefigurative, that Old Testament Jews were immoral and unfaithful but nevertheless superior to the pagans, and that the Jews were being punished specifically for killing Christ. Chrysostom's unique contribution to the history of Christian anti-Judaism stemmed from his bitter and very personal attacks on Jews. For most patristic writers, "the Jews" were largely an abstraction, a literary motif. To Chrysostom, however, the Jews were flesh and blood enemies; he saw them as demonic wolves bent on devouring his flock. The synagogue was the "synagogue of Satan," and judaizers had made a pact with the Devil. For him the implication was clear: to love Christ is to hate Jews. The medieval tendency to demonize Jews—to portray them in art and prose as akin to Satan—had many sources, but for thirteenth-century theologians, John Chrysostom was one of the most important.

Augustine, Jerome, and Chrysostom were Thomas Aquinas's favorite patristic authorities.[18] In Augustine, Aquinas had the writings of a Church Father who was relatively tolerant toward Jews and who believed they had an important, ongoing role to play in the drama of sacred history. In Jerome, he encountered a Father who combined openness to Jewish scholarship with a deep personal hostility toward Jews. Finally, in John Chrysostom, Aquinas was exposed to the most unequivocally anti-Jewish writer of the patristic age. In addition to his broad erudition and astonishing talent for analysis and synthesis, Thomas possessed the good fortune to live in an age when the treasures of Greek theology as well as Greek philosophy were at last being transmitted to the Latin West. Thus he was able to develop his ideas on Judaism and the Jews with the aid of the entire spectrum of patristic thought.

2. The Thirteenth-Century Context

By 1250, when Thomas Aquinas began his career as a mendicant in the Dominican Order, Jews had lived in western Europe time out of mind. Saint Paul wrote to Jewish Christians at Rome in the middle of the first century, and when Constantine died in 337 there was a Jewish settlement at Cologne. Jews immigrated to Moslem Spain in the eighth and ninth centuries and came to England in the aftermath of the Norman Conquest. By the thirteenth century, they were a small but seemingly permanent demographic presence in western Europe. They were also highly visible, a fact reflected in the inordinate attention they received in chronicles, royal documents, and legal codes. Jews were conspicuous for one reason: aside from the Moslems in Christian Spain, they were the only tolerated *infideles* in western Europe.

Jewish settlement in Europe was concentrated in the south, in Sicily, the Kingdom of Naples, and the Midi. In southern Italy in the thirteenth century there is evidence of at least two dozen Jewish communities, ranging in size from ten to one hundred households, and undoubtedly there were other communities whose records have been lost. Provence and Sicily also had significant Jewish populations. North of these regions, Jewish settlement was sparser. There were Jewish communities in major cities such as London and Paris, and regions such as Normandy, Anjou, and Maine also had a handful of settlements. In northern Europe, the Rhineland had the largest concentration of Jews. Worms, Speyer, and Cologne, each with Jewish communities of two to four hundred households, were the most important centers, and there were dozens of smaller Rhenish Jewries. Large parts of northern Europe, however, had no Jewish presence at all. At the time of the 1290 expulsion, for instance, there were only twenty-one communities in all of England. In the north the general picture is of a small, scattered, predominately urban population, while in southern Europe, Jewish settlement was relatively denser and perhaps more rural.[1]

Despite their small numbers, European Jews played a vital role in the medieval economy, especially before 1100. In sharp contrast to the Christian population, Jews as a group were literate and relatively cosmopolitan. European Jews frequently corresponded with relatives in Spain or the Middle East, and eminent rabbis received requests for their opinion on difficult legal matters from distant locals; Maimonides, living in Cairo in the 1190s, received an inquiry from a convert in Provence. Literary skills and international contacts enabled Jews to carve out a vital social niche. Throughout Europe, bishops and wealthy laymen routinely consulted Jewish physicians. Jewish merchants played an important role in commerce, especially in the luxury trade, thanks largely to their contacts in Spain and the Middle East. Wealthy Jews also provided venture capital for trading voyages and occasionally loaned sizable sums to princes and monasteries. Eminent Jews were sometimes employed as clerks, tax collectors, or salaried officials in the emerging political bureaucracies, though this was more common in Spain than in France, England, or the Empire. But prior to 1100, most European Jews were not bureaucrats, physicians, or international merchants. Nor were they farmers, though in Provence, southern Italy, and even northern Europe some Jews worked the land. Instead, the majority were artisans and shopkeepers. Here too their role was valuable. In an overwhelmingly agricultural economy, they provided some manufactured goods and helped expedite local trade. Jewish pawnbrokers also provided a source of small-scale consumer credit.

As a tolerated but often resented minority, Jewish communities were heavily dependant on the good will of the political authorities. One of the few safe generalizations that can be made about medieval Jewish history is that wherever Jews were protected and not burdened with oppressive taxation, they prospered. Despite some significant exceptions, most European Jews enjoyed such conditions until the late twelfth century. Jews everywhere were under the protection of the secular or ecclesiastical authorities. Crimes against Jews were tried in the courts of the king, prince, or bishop. The development in the first half of the thirteenth century of the legal doctrine that Jews were *servi camerae*, serfs of the chamber, merely formalized what had long been a social reality. Within their own communities, however, Jews were granted considerable autonomy. Local elders could punish crimes, collect tithes and taxes, control immigration, and expel troublemakers. In Germany, some communities were even allowed to confiscate the property of Jews who converted to Christianity.

In exchange for protection and local autonomy, Jews were required to pay a variety of taxes. Most important was a special tax levied on Jews alone and usually payable to the crown. This tax often had its origins in the founding of a Jewish community, or in the aftermath of a change in political authority. It was explicitly a quid pro quo: Jews were allowed to live, work, and exercise certain rights of self-government for a fixed period of time, usually three to ten years, in exchange for a fee. At the end of this period both the fee and the nature of the community's privileges were subject to change. This "Jew tax" was frequently exorbitant—in some places it generated up to 10 percent of the ruler's total revenue—but it was also relatively stable.

Because they were protected, semi-autonomous, and relatively prosperous, the history of the Jews in western Europe well into the twelfth century is characterized by growth and cultural achievement. In the eleventh century European or "Ashkenazic" Jews began to produce individuals to rival the intellectual giants of Sephardic (Spanish and Middle Eastern) Jewry. Rashi, or Rabbi Solomon Yizhaki of Troyes (1040–1105), a Talmudic scholar and biblical exegete, founded a distinctly Ashkenazic approach to the sacred texts of Judaism. His methods, which emphasized the historical context and literal meanings of scripture, were further developed by his twelfth-century successors in France and Germany, the Tosafists. In Germany, the Hasdai Ashkenaz movement combined mysticism with legal rigorism, a synthesis best expressed in the anonymous *Sefer Hasidim*. This cultural flowering among northern European Jews was accompanied by increased contact with Christian intellectuals. In Paris, for instance, Andrew of St. Victor regularly discussed problems of scriptural interpretation with Jewish exegetes, and he borrowed from Rashi in composing his own biblical commentaries.[2] Nor was the exchange of ideas entirely one-sided; the methods of the Tosafists have clear parallels with those of Christian scholasticism. Of course, social intercourse was not restricted to intellectuals. Jewish quarters had long existed, but many Jews lived outside them, and Christians sometimes lived on Jewish streets.[3] Jews and Christians alike spoke the vernacular tongue, and they interacted daily in a variety of social and economic settings.

But there were portents of change. The slaughter of thousands of Rhineland Jews in 1096 by Christian mobs caught up in the frenzied enthusiasm of the First Crusade gave dramatic testimony that suspicion and hatred often lay just below the surface. However valuable the Jews' economic role, and however cordial day-to-day contacts might be, the potential for conflict was always there. And given the small population and wholly dependent status of Europe's Jewish communities, the outcome of such conflicts was rarely in doubt.

The religious chasm between Christians and Jews was unbridgeable, and in an age that knew nothing of liberal tolerance, it inevitably produced hostility. For Christians, Jews were eternal strangers. The dietary regulations of the Mosaic Law severely limited the opportunity for Christians and Jews to engage in that most basic act of fellowship, the sharing of food. Confessional differences precluded intermarriage, so there were no family bonds to mitigate religious tensions. Jews worshipped on Friday evening and Saturday, and their language of worship was Hebrew, a mysterious tongue which inspired awe and fear among Christians. Many Christians believed that Hebrew was the primeval language spoken by Adam and Eve, but it was also regarded as the language of magic and sorcery. Its written symbols, visible on synagogues, tombstones, and documents, appeared cryptic and frightening. The rhythms of spoken Hebrew also inspired unease among Christians, as medieval legislation prohibiting loud chanting in synagogues attests. At every Christian festival, Jews were conspicuous by their absence. They were alien to the world of belief, symbol, and ritual which bound Christians in community. And because they were outsiders by choice, there was always the suspicion that Jews held the Christian creed and cult in contempt.

Absent an ideal of tolerance, an increase in religious conviction is apt to generate persecution. This is precisely what happened in medieval Europe. The Middle Ages are sometimes called the "age of faith," but prior to the twelfth century this characterization is not accurate. Outside the monasteries, Christianity was a superficial veneer on a society that was Germano-Roman in law and pagan in its cultural ideals. Europe became ideologically and culturally Christian only in the High Middle Ages, after enormous intellectual effort and institutional development. The Gregorian reforms, the crusading movement, the titanic struggles between empire and papacy, and the intellectual renaissance of the twelfth and thirteenth centuries all contributed to the christianization of European society.

Predictably, this process had adverse affects on the Jewish communities of western Europe. Made conspicuous by their dissenting status, Jews tended to suffer most when the drive for Christian unity and expansion was at high tide. "Can it please God that we go to slay the infidel in distant lands, while leaving the infidel in our midst unmolested?" asked one monk while preaching the First Crusade. The tremendous energies released in the efforts to conquer the Holy Land repeatedly spilled over into violence against the Jews. Later, the medieval Inquisition regarded the Jews with deep suspicion. Judaism was seen as a font of heresy, and the Waldensians in particular, with their iconoclasm and rejection of the invocation of saints, were thought by many to be judaizers.[4] More generally, it was assumed that Jews, because they were infidels themselves, had a natural sympathy for the heterodox. Inquisitors often accused Jews of giving succor to heretical Christians as well as encouraging converts to abandon their new faith and revert to Judaism.

Economic changes exacerbated the pressures on the Jews. Paradoxically, the expansion of the European economy after 1100 actually diminished the economic opportunities of Jews, at least in the long run. As trade between Europe and the Byzantine empire expanded, Christian merchants in Italian cities such as Genoa and Venice gradually established commercial dominance. This new avenue of east-west trade undermined the value of the Jews' international contacts. They were not entirely excluded from commerce, but their role became marginal. The growth of towns and the development of a Christian artisan class also isolated the Jews. As artisans banded together in guilds to control wages, prices, and quality, they modeled themselves on the corporate organizations they were most familiar with—cathedral chapters and monasteries. These guilds were sometimes referred to as *ecclesiae*, and, almost always, a formal Christian oath was required for membership. As a result, Jewish craftsmen were increasingly allowed to offer their goods only within the limited market of the Jewish community.

By the middle of the twelfth century, there is evidence that northern European Jews were channeling their remaining capital into the most profitable avenue left to them: loaning money at interest. Powerful forces were pushing Jews in this direction. Not only were other ways of earning profits being closed to them, but in the expanding European economy there was an insatiable demand for venture capital and consumer credit. Kings required cash to pay their soldiers and bureaucrats; merchants sought financing for trading voyages; farmers and burgurs, pressed by inflation and enticed by consumer goods, needed money to pay their bills and buy the things they wanted. Jews with capital were uniquely able to provide for these needs. Mosaic law permitted them to loan money at interest to non-Jews, while both civil and canon law prohibited Christians from practicing "usury." Of course, many Christians violated this prohibition; merchants found ingenious ways of hiding interest in artificially inflated prices, and entire cities, such as Cahors, were notorious centers of usury. But moral scruples and the force of law did inhibit lending among Christians. As a result, borrowers often turned to Jewish lenders when they needed funds. Monarchs and bishops sometimes sought out wealthy Jews for loans to fund major construction projects or overcome a shortfall in revenue. Much more commonly, Jews of modest means loaned small sums to peasants and townsmen, usually taking a pledge as security.

European Jews had little choice but to turn to moneylending, and Jewish lenders and pawnbrokers performed a vital economic function. But the results of this trend were disastrous.

Consumer loans were the source of most of the trouble. When peasants and townsmen needed cash to make a purchase or pay an overdue bill, they often borrowed money from Jews, providing some object of value as security for the loan. Frequently the borrower was not able to pay back the loan in full within the requisite period. This was due to a number of factors, primarily the sterile nature of consumer credit and the high interest—often 20 to 50 percent—borne by such loans as a result of the general shortage of cash in the medieval economy. When this happened, the term of the loan was usually extended, with an added penalty for not paying it off on time. Often the borrower was unable to meet the terms of the extended loan either. When this happened he had the bitter experience of seeing his pledge sold after he had made interest payments and even paid back part of the principle.

As more Jews began lending money at interest in the twelfth and thirteenth centuries, such experiences became common. *Iudaeus* became a synonym for *usurarius*, and the phrase "to judaize" was sometimes used to refer to the practice of usury rather than the incorporation of Jewish elements into Christian belief or ritual.[5] Christian theologians unanimously condemned "excessive" interest, and some thirteenth-century scholastics—including Thomas Aquinas—adopted the extreme position that *all* interest constituted usury. Ordinary Christians, already suspicious of Jews because of their unbelief and social exclusivity, came to regard them as economic parasites who lived off the labor of others rather than working to support themselves. Kings and princes, always eager to augment their income, took advantage of this perception: beginning in the late twelfth century, Philip Augustus of France and other rulers began staging *captiones* or seizures of Jewish property. These confiscatory raids were justified on the grounds that Jewish wealth had been acquired through usury. Rulers who for decades had enforced loan contracts and taxed their profits were suddenly shocked to discover that the Jews of their realm had been practicing usury.[6]

Economic hostility toward medieval Jews was not merely the result of popular resentment, scholastic theory, or political opportunism, however; its ultimate sources were rooted in the Christian mentality. Medieval

Christians were deeply ambivalent about money and commercial exchange. After all, Saint Paul had declared that money was the root of all evil. Yet in the new market economy of twelfth- and thirteenth-century Europe, money and commercial exchange were increasingly important; more than ever, human relations seemed to be governed by cold calculation and economic self-interest rather than Christian love. In this context, the increasing involvement of Jews in moneylending provided a convenient scapegoat.[7] Money was intrinsically unclean, and making it through lending and exchange rather than through visible labor seemed exploitative and dishonest. Dealing with money also involved written documents and complex calculations of interest, both of which seemed suspicious to the verbally and mathematically illiterate masses of Christian Europe.

Religious and economic factors combined to create the stereotypical Jew of popular belief. Because Christians were convinced that Jews were usurers whose stock in trade was dealing with tainted lucre, they thought of them as dishonest, scheming, and unclean. These vices dovetailed nicely with the demonic qualities Christians attributed to Jews because of their role in the execution of Jesus. As pharasaical Christ-killers, Jews were perceived as malevolent and disloyal, impious and cruel. Iconography fused these attributes: the Jew's grasping hands and a sack of coins symbolized greed, while large ears, a recessive chin, and a long hooked nose provided visual links with popular images of Satan. Other motifs were even more ominous: one popular image depicted a Jew sucking the teats of a sow, while another showed a Jewish moneylender stretching out his hands to receive gold from the anus of a monster.[8]

Religious beliefs, economic changes, popular stereotypes, and the essentially powerless status of European Jews all helped to determine their fate in the thirteenth century. The canon law of the Catholic Church also played an important role. By the thirteenth century a comprehensive body of codified ecclesiastical law had been developed which, in theory, regulated the status of Jews in western Christendom and limited their contacts with Christians. The various canons were motivated by two not entirely compatible goals: to preserve and protect the Jews who served as witnesses to the truth of the Gospel and whose eventual conversion was promised in sacred writ, and to insure that Jews were segregated and degraded in order to preserve Christians from doctrinal contagion and show conclusively that God had rejected the Jews.

In developing its canon law, as in so much else, the medieval papacy looked to the ancient Roman Empire as its model and inspiration. Just as

Roman Emperors had promulgated universal laws and attempted to impose order on a vast realm through a hierarchical bureaucracy, so medieval popes, with their dream of *plenitudo potestatis* and a Christian imperium, attempted to transform bishops and priests into bureaucrats of a universal Church and to force secular rulers to do their bidding as well. This grand design was never entirely translated into reality, of course, but in the thirteenth century it still seemed it might be. In any case, what is surprising is not that the medieval papacy failed to achieve its most ambitious goals, but that—given its lack of coercive power—it achieved as much as it did.[9]

Justice was the medieval papacy's most precious commodity, for its other means of enforcing its will had serious shortcomings. Moral exhortation was notoriously ineffective. Excommunication, interdict, and crusade were more powerful weapons, but a determined opponent could stand up to them—as King John of England proved by retaining his throne during the interdict of 1208 to 1213—and if used too often they lost their value: in the 1240s the pious Louis IX of France simply ignored Innocent IV's call for a crusade against the Holy Roman Emperor, Frederick II.

In the rapidly changing social and economic climate of medieval Europe, however, justice was in high demand. As men competed for control of valuable lands and lucrative secular and ecclesiastical offices, a litigious society was born. Much of this legal business was handled by local secular and ecclesiastical courts, and in fact such institutions also experienced explosive growth in the twelfth and thirteenth centuries. But as an international institution with high moral prestige, the papacy was in a uniquely strategic position to serve as an appellate court for dissatisfied litigants. The "papal monarchy" that developed in the late twelfth and early thirteenth century was largely judicial in its structure and powers, and its efforts to shape Europe into a unified Christian society generally took the form of promulgating laws and intervening in disputes.

One part of the vision of Christendom enshrined in canon law was the conception of the status and role of Jews outlined above. Medieval popes promulgated scores of laws regulating the Jews and their relations with Christians, then used exhortation, threats, and their power as appellate judges to enforce them. The popes did not always get their way, but again what is most surprising is the extent to which canon law shaped the treatment of the Jews in Christian Europe.

In attempting to regulate the status of Jews in Europe, the popes followed in the footsteps of the Roman Emperors of the fourth and fifth centuries.[10] After the conversion of Constantine to Christianity in 313, and the gradual christianization of the empire in the course of the fourth century, Roman Law—codified in the Theodosian Code of 439 and Justinian's Code of 534—began to deal with questions presented by the presence of the Jews from a specifically Christian perspective. The policy that developed was not entirely novel. Jews had for centuries been treated as a tolerated religious minority within the Roman empire, and here the status quo was essentially preserved. Emperors continued to view the protection of true religion as one of their duties—Christianity had simply replaced the Roman pantheon as the state religion—and they continued to allow the Jews, a distinct and ancient *populus*, considerable religious freedom and legal autonomy. But the fact that Christianity was now the favored religion did produce some changes. Previously the ban on Gentile circumcision—a measure designed to discourage conversions to Judaism—had been the only statute regulating religious and social intercourse between Romans and Jews. Under the Christian imperium, however, laws were promulgated which aimed at carefully controlling such contacts, in accord with the Church's theological purposes. Thus in the fourth and fifth centuries Jews were excluded from holding civil offices that would entail exercising power over Christians. They were also forbidden to own Christian slaves. Mixed marriages were outlawed, and conversion to Judaism was defined as apostasy and made punishable by death. Like the ban on circumcision promulgated by the pagan empire, these laws were designed to prevent conversion to Judaism. The new statutes made it clear, however, that the state was much more concerned with Jewish proselytizing than it had been in the pre-Christian period; emperors now sought not only to prevent the overt acts of circumcision and conversion, but also to inhibit relationships and social contacts which might make conversion possible. Other laws sought to insure that social reality corresponded to the Christian view of Judaism as a lifeless relic. Jews were forbidden to seek converts from paganism as well as among Christians, and building or repairing a synagogue became a crime. Roman law even attempted to censor the Talmud, thus providing an imperial precedent for similar efforts by thirteenth-century popes.[11]

Even before the Christian empire began attempting to regulate Jewish-Christian relations, preachers, bishops, and Church councils were doing the same thing. John Chrysostom's *Sermons Against Judaizing Christians* are the most notorious example of a Christian warning against even casual social contact with Jews, but there were many others. Origen, Tertullian, and Jerome all urged ordinary Christians to avoid discussing religion with Jews, and around 310 the Council of Elvira warned Christians against eating and drinking with them.[12]

Judaism was, at least in some areas, a missionary religion well into the fourth century, and—like the laws promulgated by the Emperors—patristic warnings against social contacts with Jews were primarily intended to shield Christians from the danger of apostasy. To some extent this theme endured. Because the Christian church accepted the Hebrew scriptures as canonical, there was always the possibility that a learned Jew could convince a Christian that Jesus of Nazareth did not fulfill the messianic prophecies contained in those scriptures. And in fact it seems likely that until the eleventh century more Christians converted to Judaism than the reverse.[13] There was also justifiable fear that Jews who did accept Christianity might return to their ancestral faith.

With the eclipse of Judaism as a proselytizing faith, however, conversion to Judaism became a secondary concern. The popes and other churchmen did not stop worrying about the possibility of Jews seducing Christians into apostasy, but other aims became paramount: segregating and degrading Jews so that there should be no doubt that they had been rejected by God; preserving them as an artifact testifying to the truth of Christianity; and converting them to the Christian faith. Some preachers and bishops, such as Agobard of Lyons in the ninth century and Pope Leo VII in the tenth, stressed the degradation and conversion themes to the point of calling for the expulsion of Jews from specific areas when they refused to accept baptism.[14] More influential in the long run, however, was the relatively moderate attitude of Pope Gregory the Great.[15]

Aside from Leo I, Gregory (590–604) was the only early pope subsequently regarded as a Church Father. His *Pastoral Rule*, his *Moralia in Job*, and his many extant letters had an enormous influence on Latin Christianity. In these writings, Gregory almost always refers to Jews in harsh and negative terms. For Gregory, the Jews are blind, stubborn, and arrogant. Above all, they are "carnal"; that is, they are so concerned with the literal sense of scripture that they cannot comprehend its deeper spiritual meanings.

Gregory never doubted that Jews in a Christian society should be controlled and degraded. He firmly opposed the practice of Jews possessing Christian slaves, and he denied Jews had any right to proselytize among Christians or pagans. At the same time, however, Gregory believed they should be tolerated within certain limits. He stressed that their persons and property should not be violated, even in order to effect their conversion. Jewish proselytizing must be prohibited, yet Jews should be allowed to worship in peace. On one occasion Gregory sharply rebuked a Jewish convert to Christianity who incited a mob to violate a synagogue.

Notably, his calls for tolerance were not explicitly based on theological considerations, but on humanitarian grounds. He urged Christians to treat Jews with kindness and compassion rather than with hatred and violence, arguing that such an attitude both was demanded by the Gospel and would be more effective in leading the Jews to accept Christianity. In sum, Gregory believed Jews should be protected but kept in their place. He expressed this idea in an enormously influential formulation: "Just as the Jews ought not be allowed to do more in their synagogues than the law allows them, so too they should suffer no reduction in the privileges previously granted them."[16]

For the next four centuries, Gregory's attitude had little influence on the Jewish policies either of his successors or of western European monarchs. Throughout this period, most secular rulers were remarkably tolerant of Jews. Bernard Bachrach has shown that between 481 and 850 only a handful of monarchs issued so much as a single anti-Jewish decree, while many more encouraged Jewish immigration and granted privileges to Jewish communities.[17] Louis the Pious, for instance, maintained a firmly tolerant stance despite the calls of Agobard of Lyons and other churchmen for a harsh anti-Jewish policy. Throughout this period, the popes made little effort to influence the treatment of European Jews, though documents issued by Stephen III (768–772) and Leo VII (937–939) give evidence of a suspicious and hostile attitude. From the time of Gregory the Great through the eleventh century, however, "there existed no articulated [papal] program for dealing with the Jews."[18]

This changed during the pontificate of Calixtus II (1119–1124), with his promulgation of the "Constitution for the Jews," *Sicut Iudaeis*. This document was reissued some twenty times over the next three centuries and in 1234 was included in a definitive collection of canon law, the *Decretales* of Pope Gregory IX. Taking its opening sentence and basic principle from the statement of Gregory the Great quoted above, *Sicut* provided the first systematic statement of papal Jewish policy. It is worth quoting from at length.

> Just as the Jews ought not be allowed to do more in their synagogues than the law permits, so too they should suffer no reduction in the privileges that have been previously granted them. That is why, though they prefer to remain obstinate rather than acknowledge the words of the prophets and the secrets of their own scriptures and come to a knowledge of Christianity and salvation, because they have sought our protection and aid, and in accordance with the mercy of Christian piety . . . we grant them their petition and offer them

> our shield of protection. We also decree (*statuimus*) that no Christian shall use violence to force them to be baptized if they are reluctant or unwilling; but if any of them seeks refuge among Christians because of his faith, after his willingness has been made clear, he shall become a Christian without suffering any calumny. For it is impossible to believe that one who comes to baptism unwillingly truly possesses the Christian faith.
>
> Also, absent due authority, no Christian shall presume to harm them, kill them, take their money, or alter the privileges they have become accustomed to in that region. In addition, during the celebration of their festivals, no one should assault them with sticks or stones, nor should any services be required of them except those which have long been customary. And, in opposition to the depravity and avarice of evil men, we decree that no one shall desecrate or diminish Jewish cemeteries or, with the object of extorting money, exhume those buried there. If, however—God forbid—someone knowingly acts in defiance of this decree, he shall suffer loss of honor and office, or be restrained by excommunication, until he makes satisfaction.
>
> We wish, however, to place under the protection of this decree only those who have not presumed to plot in subversion of the Christian faith.[19]

A number of points about *Sicut* should be noted. First, the bull was addressed to "all the Christian faithful" and—at least in the first instance—it was issued at the request of a group of unnamed Jews. Jews had appealed to the pope for protection, and in response he issued a "constitution" intended to be binding for all Christians. Such an action clearly presupposed a vastly expanded conception of papal powers; whereas previous popes had mainly sought to influence the policies of secular rulers, Calixtus II and his successors arrogated to themselves the authority of extending direct protection to the Jews of Europe. Second, *Sicut* not only insured the rights of Jews, it also berated them for their failure to acknowledge Christ. Protection and condemnation go hand in hand; both are means to a fundamentally theological end. Third, the bull granted specific privileges, privileges that the Jews had long enjoyed but now found threatened: protection from physical harm, theft, and forced conversion; freedom of worship; limited taxation; and preservation of Jewish cemeteries. Finally, *Sicut* contained loopholes. It guaranteed basic privileges only to those Jews "who do not plot to subvert the Christian faith" ("qui nihil machinari presumpserit in subversionem fidei christiane"). Also, the property and person of Jews who violated secular laws were not protected. Though entirely justified in their original context—Calixtus could hardly be expected to protect criminals or Jews who actively sought to undermine the Church—these loopholes made it possible for those with a special animus against Jews to attack them without violating the letter of *Sicut*. The charge that Jews sought to undermine Christianity enabled the Inquisition to extend its authority over Jews suspected of aiding heretics or urging Jewish converts to return to their ancestral faith, while secular laws prohibiting usury were used to justify expelling the Jews from France in 1182 and 1304 and from England in 1290.

Despite its limitations, *Sicut* was born of a sincere desire on the part of the medieval papacy to protect the Jews from wanton violence and persecution. As noted, thirteenth- and fourteenth-century popes frequently reissued the bull, usually in response to Jewish requests, and it was included in the *Decretales*, a papally approved collection of canon law promulgated in 1234. The *Sicut* principle was also extended to new contingencies. In 1247, Pope Innocent IV added an appendix to *Sicut* which strongly condemned the "ritual murder" charge (the claim that Jews crucified a Christian child as part of their Passover ritual and mixed its blood with their *matzoth*).[20] Gregory X did the same in 1272, arguing that those who made such charges actually sought to plunder the Jews and pointing out that it was impossible for Jews to partake of human blood, as even animal blood was forbidden them by the Mosaic Law. He went on to demand the release of all who had been accused of such a crime.[21] Later, amidst the hysteria of 1348, Clement VI defended Jews from the charge that they had intentionally spread the Black Death.

> This plague has struck different parts of the world, both amid the Jews themselves and also among other nations where Jews do not dwell at all. It is absolutely unthinkable that the aforesaid Jews have performed so terrible a deed.[22]

But *Sicut* was just part of the story. The popes' ultimate goal was to shape European society in accord with a theological vision, a vision which required Jewish existence but that also demanded their segregation and oppression. During the long period of papal impotence in western Europe (roughly 400 to 1000), many rulers had instituted policies favorable to Jews. Some Jews served as royal officials and tax collectors; others were permitted to own Christian slaves. In both cases, infidel Jews exercised *dominium* over Christians. In addition, some rulers actually impeded missionary work by allowing Jewish communities to confiscate the property of converts. Medieval popes were scandalized by these situations. Christians were the chosen of God, and it was intolerable that Jews should exercise authority over them or prevent other Jews from adopting the true faith. As Innocent III declared in 1205, "the perfidious Jews should in no way become insolent, but rather under the fear of slavery should always be made aware of their guilt and be forced to honor the Christian faith."[23]

In pursuit of this policy, medieval popes reaffirmed the entire range of Roman law restrictions on the Jews. Dozens of canons in Gratian's *Decretum*, Gregory IX's *Decretales*, and other compilations of canon law were designed to limit and control the activities of Jews and to guard against dangerous contacts between Jews and Christians.[24] Laws were promulgated which prohibited Jews from owning Christian slaves, employing Christian nurses, or holding offices that would involve exercising authority over Christians. They were not allowed to proselytize, they could not build new synagogues or repair old ones, and in their worship they were to refrain from loud chanting. During Holy Week Jews were not to appear in public. This rule was designed partly to protect Jews from Christian violence, but it had other purposes as well: The sixty-eighth canon of the Fourth Lateran Council in 1215 decreed that "they shall not appear in public on the days of lamentation for the Lord's Passion, for we have heard that some of them do not blush to go about dressed ornately on such days and to ridicule Christians who display signs of grief in memory of the most sacred Passion."[25] In order to make them more conspicuous, the same council also decreed that Jews should be recognizable by their clothing. This canon led to the implementation of the notorious "Jewish badge" in Christian countries, a policy the Moslems had adopted several centuries earlier. On their side, Christians were not to consult Jewish doctors, marry Jews, or even share a meal with them. Above all, Christians were not to discuss religion with Jews. Disputations were to be held only under ecclesiastical auspices, with qualified disputants and in situations where there was no danger of a Jew getting the better of the argument.[26]

Like the laws promulgated by the Christian empire, medieval papal policy extended limited protections to Jews while simultaneously working to make them social outcasts. But there was an important difference between imperial and papal efforts to control the status of Jews in western Europe: the papal program was vastly more effective. In the main, the Roman laws had been issued during the twilight of imperial power in western Europe. Hence these laws had little impact on Jewish communities in places such as Italy, France, and Germany. Canon law, by contrast, both reflected and contributed to the growth of papal power in the High Middle Ages. Unlike the late emperors, the popes were in a position to enforce their will in western Europe.

To be sure, there was always slippage between the vision and social reality. Secular rulers had agendas of their own, agendas that might include but were never limited to the Church's policies. During periods of strife between Rome and the German emperors, for instance, the Staufers and Hohenstaufens often ignored the wishes of the papacy. And the popes themselves were not entirely consistent. Papal Jewish policy demanded a delicate balance between protection and oppression, and it is not surprising that some popes failed to maintain the equilibrium. In 1146, for instance, Pope Eugenius III did virtually nothing to protect German Jews from the anti-Jewish pogroms that accompanied the Second Crusade. On the other hand, most popes made only sporadic efforts to enforce the wearing of the "Jewish badge," and the papal position on moneylending was notoriously inconsistent; theologians and secular rulers were often more vigorous in their condemnation of the Jews as usurers than were the bishops of Rome.[27] Also, maintaining a consistent Jewish policy was only one of many papal concerns. Often the popes simply had bigger fish to fry. But when all is said and done, the fact remains that a remarkably detailed body of canon law concerning the Jews was promulgated in the High Middle Ages, and the various popes made a concerted effort to insure their decrees were obeyed.

In theory, ecclesiastical hegemony over European Jews was circumscribed by the canonistic principle *de his qui foris sunt*. Based on I Corinthians 5.12–13, this principle stated that the pope had no direct authority over the internal affairs of non-Christians. As a result, all papal legislation affecting non-Christians had to be justified on one of two grounds: (1) the laws were promulgated by the pope in his role as secular ruler rather than as head of the Catholic Church, or (2) the laws were designed to protect the Christian faith from attack or disparagement. According to this principle, the pope could use segregation and other measures to protect Christians from the "perfidious" influence of the Jews, but he could not intervene directly in the internal affairs of Jewish communities. Until the 1230s, the popes adhered to this principle. Medieval European society has been called totalitarian, and in some ways the charge is justified, but it is a remarkable fact that for many centuries both Church and state not only tolerated infidel Jews but also allowed them limited self-government and a high degree of religious liberty.

As the doctrine of *plenitudo potestatis* was developed and refined in the thirteenth century, however, *foris* became vulnerable. *Plenitudo potestatis* is the doctrine that universal sovereignty, both spiritual and temporal, was given to Peter by Christ—sovereignty over all human beings, not just Christians. Clearly expressed by Sinibaldo Fieschi (Pope Innocent IV) in his commentary on the *Decretales* of Gregory IX and eventually given its most famous expression by Boniface VIII in the bull *Unam Sanctam* in 1302, the doctrine made it theoretically possible to justify papal intervention into the internal affairs of the Jewish people.[28]

In the 1230s the papacy began doing just that. But the popes were not the first ecclesiastical officials to intervene in the internal religious affairs of the Jews. Ironically, the Church first violated Jewish religious autonomy when a group of Jews in Provence asked the local Dominicans to take action in the "Maimonides controversy," a dispute between Provençal rabbis and others who believed Maimonides' philosophical speculations had led him into heresy, and his defenders, mostly Spanish intellectuals, who claimed his writings were compatible with orthodox Judaism. Subsequent generations had many occasions to lament that act. Eagerly seizing the opportunity, Dominicans in southern France examined Maimonides' writings and publicly burned some of them in 1232.[29]

For the time being, the episode remained an isolated one. But it was a portent of things to come. A number of forces were converging which would soon lead the Church to adopt a more invasive attitude toward Judaism. The increasingly grandiose conception of papal prerogatives has already been noted. In addition, awareness of Judaism as a religion with a vigorous, living tradition—rather than the ossified artifact of Christian ideology—was on the rise. In the mid-twelfth century, a significant number of Christian scholars began learning Hebrew. Some went on to translate Hebrew scientific and philosophical texts into Latin; others began consulting works of rabbinic exegesis as an aid to writing their own biblical commentaries. In time, Christian Hebraists turned their attention to the Talmud, the ancient compilation of rabbinic law which was the spiritual cornerstone of medieval Judaism. Awareness of the Talmud and other Jewish writings made it possible for scholars to have a richer understanding of Judaism, but for Jews this development was fraught with peril. The Talmud had been compiled and commented on after the advent of Christianity, and in the process of explicating the Law and defending the truth of Judaism, the various sages and commentators had criticized and occasionally disparaged the Christian faith. Both churchmen and lay Christians felt they had treated Jews with great kindness—after all, they had tolerated them even though the Jews were cursed and dangerous infidels—and they felt betrayed when they discovered that Jews had been mocking them for centuries.

More generally, Jewish religious freedom and autonomy was the victim of medieval Europe's drive for system, uniformity, and expansion. In the mid-thirteenth century, the same impulse that produced the Crusades and the violent suppression of the Albigensian heresy began to focus upon the Jews, Europe's most obvious group of religious dissidents. Just as medieval Europe's economic growth was both external and internal, encompassing the expansion of the arable and the growth of international commerce as well increased internal trade and the development of more productive agricultural techniques, so too ideological expansion had its external and internal modes. While crusaders besieged the Holy Land and missionaries sought converts abroad, the papacy, the Inquisition, and the mendicant orders worked to eradicate heresy and establish a religiously uniform society. The Church's efforts to convert, or at least more effectively control, European Jews was but a small part of this comprehensive effort.

In 1236, a converted Jew, Nicholas Donin, presented Pope Gregory IX with a list of charges against the Talmud, the Jewish liturgy, and collections of Midrash. Donin claimed that these works blasphemed Christ and the Virgin Mary and permitted Jews to practice deception, theft, and violence against Christians. He also informed the pope that the Talmud was regarded by the Jews as superior in authority to the Mosaic Law. As a result, Donin claimed, Jews were largely ignorant of the authentic Hebrew scriptures and the testimony they bore to the truth of Christianity. After a three-year delay, Gregory responded to these charges. He sent Donin to William of Auvergne, the bishop of Paris, with a letter instructing William to command the kings of France, England, Aragon, and Castile to confiscate all Jewish books on the first Sabbath of the following Lent (March 3, 1240) and hand them over to the Dominicans and Franciscans. The Dominican and Franciscan priors in Paris were authorized to destroy any books found to contain blasphemy or doctrinal error.

Only Louis IX of France complied with this order, and before proceeding against the Jewish books he allowed Rabbi Yehiel ben Joseph the opportunity to defend them before a tribunal of clerics. The outcome was never in doubt. The Talmud and other works were found to contain heretical and blasphemous passages. In 1242 twenty-four wagon loads of Jewish books were consigned to the flames.[30]

Yet papal policy on the Talmud soon changed. Innocent IV (1243–1254), at first a strong supporter of the campaign against the Talmud, reversed himself in 1247 and ordered copies of the work returned to the Jews.[31] Subsequent popes were equally inconsistent. Though the Talmud was subjected to sporadic ecclesiastical censorship over the next three centuries, no perpetually binding canon against it was ever promulgated.[32] Nevertheless, the Talmud trial and the Inquisition's role in the Maimonides controversy established an important precedent: In both cases representatives of the Catholic Church had examined and condemned Hebrew books written by and for Jews. Technically, the *foris* principle still held, since the Talmud as well as the writings of Maimonides had been condemned on the grounds of blaspheming the Christian faith, encouraging Jews to harm Christians, and interfering with Christian missionary efforts. But its effectiveness as a guarantor of Jewish religious autonomy had been seriously undermined.

Rather than additional attacks, the next few decades witnessed the development of a different, though equally intrusive, approach to Jewish literature: missionaries began using selected passages from the Talmud and other Jewish religious works to build a case for the truth of Christianity. Once again the innovator was a converted Jew, in this case Pablo Christiani, formerly Saul of Montpellier, who after his baptism had been received into the Dominican Order.[33]

The preaching campaign of Pablo Christiani in Provence and Aragon in the late 1250s and early 1260s represented the first serious effort by the medieval Church to convert the Jews in its midst. Eleventh- and twelfth-century theologians such as Peter Damian, Gilbert Crispin, and Peter the Venerable had contributed to the *contra Iudaeos* genre, but their polemics, which were intended primarily for Christian audiences, merely repeated the exegetical and historical arguments that Jews had considered and rejected in the fourth century.[34] Christiani did not neglect these traditional arguments in his missionary preaching, but the heart of his strategy was a carefully selected group of Talmudic and Midrashic texts. These texts, according to the former rabbinical student, proved that Jewish sages believed the Messiah had come sometime in the first century, was theanthropic, and had abrogated Mosaic Law. The inevitable conclusion—Christiani hoped—was that the Messiah was none other than Jesus of Nazareth. In his view, Jews had to either accept this fact or reject their own sacred texts.[35]

Christiani's preaching failed to win many converts. Neither Christian nor Jewish chroniclers mention any mass conversions, and Rabbi Moses ben Nachman's account of the Barcelona Disputation of 1263, where Christiani attempted to prove the truth of Christianity by using Jewish texts, fairly drips with contempt. This is hardly surprising. Despite having "a perverse appeal,"[36] Christiani's argument also had an obvious weakness, which Nachmanides was only too happy to point out: If the sages whose dicta were recorded in the Talmud believed Jesus was the Messiah, why had they remained Jews?

Despite the intrinsic shortcomings of Christiani's approach and his lack of missionary success, he continued to receive both secular and ecclesiastical support. For at least a decade, popes, princes, and the Dominican

Order did what they could to force Jews to listen to his sermons. As late as 1269 he was authorized by Louis IX to preach in a number of synagogues in and around Paris.[37] Meanwhile, others worked to refine the approach Christiani had pioneered. In the late 1260s and early 1270s, another Dominican, Raymond Marti, compiled the *Pugio Fidei* ("Dagger of Faith"), a massive collection of Talmudic and rabbinic texts accompanied by Christological glosses. This herculean work of scholarship quickly became the most important source of Christian knowledge of the Talmud and remained so for the rest of the Middle Ages. The *Pugio Fidei* circulated widely, and various preachers drew on it in giving conversionary sermons before captive audiences of Jews. Other strategies were tried as well. But nothing worked. Like the new "innovative argumentation," efforts to combine social and economic pressure with material inducements failed to produce the desired results. In spite of being segregated and despised, victimized by discriminatory economic policies and sporadic popular violence, and targeted by intense if inconsistent missionary efforts, the vast majority of European Jews held steadfastly to their faith.

It was in this context that Thomas Aquinas wrote about the Jews and their religion. Thomas came to Paris for the first time in 1244, just two years after the conclusion of the Talmud trials. He lived long enough to see the development of the new missionary strategy, which aimed at using the Talmud to convert Jews; Aquinas was in Paris when Pablo Christiani preached there in 1269, and Raymond Marti completed the *Pugio Fidei* in 1272, two years before Thomas's death. Aquinas also witnessed the growing resentment against Jewish usury expressed in two seizures or *captiones* of Jewish property in France, and he heard the arguments of radicals who called for seizing Jewish children in order to baptize them and raise them as Christians. Nor was he merely an observer. Thomas also played an active, if minor, role in shaping Jewish policy. In 1259, Raymond de Peñafort asked him to compose a work that would help missionaries in Spain convert the Jews and Moslems there, and he responded by writing the massive *Summa Contra Gentiles*. Twelve years later, he wrote a letter to Marguerite, the Countess of Flanders and daughter of King Louis IX of France, in which he responded to her inquiries concerning the proper treatment of her Jewish subjects. In his *Summa Theologiae*, Aquinas also discussed a variety of questions concerning the social and economic status of the Jews in Christian society. Finally, in both the *Summa* and in his biblical commentaries, he wrote at length on the nature of the Mosaic Law, the guilt of the Jews for the crucifixion of Jesus, and the role of the Jews in the divine plan. It is to these writings that we now turn.

3. People of the Promises, People of the Law

> Praecepta veteris legis vitalia sint, non tamen vitam habent in seipsis, sed intantum dicuntur vitalia inquantum ducunt ad Christum.
>
> —*Super Evangelium Iohannis* 5.6

For Thomas Aquinas, Christ is the axis of history. Prior to his Incarnation, only those events that prefigured or prepared the way for him had lasting importance; since his Resurrection, the spread of the Gospel and the development of Christian doctrine have been the dominant themes. Everything else—the migration of peoples, the rise and fall of empires—either draws meaning from some connection with the drama of salavation history or else is trivial, merely profane.

This conception of history explains the importance of the Jews in Aquinas's thought. He saw Jewish history as falling into two vast eras—the time under the Law and the time after the Law—with a crucial hinge in between: the period A.D. 30–70, from the beginning of Jesus' public ministry to the destruction of the Temple in Jerusalem by the Roman Emperor Titus. In each period, Aquinas believed, the Jews were an instrument of God's will and a means of his revelation. Under the Law, their life and worship was a sign of God's righteousness and a symbol of what was to come, and their history set the stage for the Incarnation. Then, in rejecting and crucifying Jesus, the Jews inadvertently fulfilled the words of the prophets and effected the sacrifice which made possible the salvation of the Gentiles. Finally, their homelessness and misery after A.D. 70—a divine punishment for their role in the Crucifixion—gives mute testimony to the justice of God and the truth of the Christian message. In this chapter and the two that follow we will analyze each stage of Aquinas's schema in turn: first, his views on the Jews' covenant relation with God, the nature of their Law, and their development as a holy people; next, their role in the Crucifixion and the nature of their guilt and punishment; and lastly the status and function of Jews in a Christian society.

Like Paul, Aquinas traced the origins of the Jewish people to the patriarch Abraham. They are his descendants *secundum carnem*—"according to the flesh"—and their increase and their conquest of Canaan fulfilled the divine promises of countless descendants and a chosen land. But for Thomas, the Abrahamic covenant was at once too narrow and too general to constitute the Jews as a *populus*. On the one hand, God promised Abraham a son whose descendants would dwell in the land to which God had led him. This was sufficient to make him the founder of a family or a tribe, but it was hardly enough to constitute a "people." Conversely, Aquinas (again following Paul) believed Abraham was more than the father of the Jews; he was the ancestor of all men of faith. In his view, the prophecies which were specifically fulfilled in the history of the Jews—the vast increase in population and the conquest of the Holy Land—constituted only a portion of what was promised. He argued that the incarnation of Christ and the establishment of a universal religion were also contained implicitly in the Abrahamic covenant. Thus Abraham is as much the father of Christians as of Jews.[1]

For Aquinas, the Law constituted the essential identity of the Jews as a holy people, set apart and consecrated to God. This follows from his Augustinian definition of a *populus* as a group that is numerous, free, and guided by a body of law ordered to the common good.[2] To him it was clear that the Jews did not obtain this status until the great theophany on Mount Sinai. Prior to their descent into Egypt, Abraham's progeny were too few in number to form a true *populus*. In Egypt their population increased, but as long as they remained slaves they could not become God's people in the full sense, for they could not receive the divine Law until they had been liberated from Egyptian rule. The Exodus was necessary not only as a first step toward the promised conquest of the Holy Land, but also so Israel could receive the Law and become a covenant people.[3]

Thomas subsumes everything in Israelite history—the promises to Abraham, the Exodus, the giving of the Law, the conquest of the Holy Land, the rise and fall of the Davidic monarchy—under the divine plan that culminated with the Incarnation. The temporal promises of descendants and a homeland given to Abraham symbolize the growth of the Church and salvation in Christ.[4] Similarly, it is legitimate to seek mystical significance in the victories and defeats of Israel's armies, whereas the military history of the Roman empire is devoid of spiritual meaning.[5] But it was in the Law that God made his fullest revelation to the Jews. Hence it is not merely licit but mandatory to look for mystical or prefigurative meanings in the Mosaic Law; those who do not fail to understand fully its significance. The Law is a kind of divine cryptogram, and the primary task of exegesis is to uncover the divine plan that lies hidden beneath—or within—the Law's precepts, to show how each commandment worked to inculcate moral and religious knowledge and to prefigure Christ, his Church, and the eternal salvation he made possible.

Thomas dealt with the Mosaic Law in a number of contexts; the *Lectures on Romans*, for example, are an especially rich source of ideas. But only in his "Treatise on the Old Law" (*Summa Theologiae, Prima Secundae* 98–105) did he attempt a synoptic treatment. Here, in a tour de force of scholastic analysis, Aquinas employed all his organizational and logical skills in an effort to bring order to the unwieldy mass of legal material contained in the Pentateuch: He divided the precepts into types and subtypes, examined the Law as a polity, a legal code, and a liturgical handbook, probed dozens of specific commandments to uncover their literal and symbolic meaning, and consulted the opinions of earlier commentators such as Jerome, Augustine, and Gregory the Great.

Aquinas was so intent on this task that he was willing to violate the structure of his crowning work, the *Summa Theologiae*. Designed as a textbook for beginners in theology, the *Summa* is divided into questions and articles. Most of the articles follow a set pattern: A problem is stated in question form, Aquinas deals with it in a one- or two-thousand-word essay, and then he replies to three or four anticipated objections. The "Treatise on the Old Law" retains the article form, and the *corpus* of the article is usually brief. But in some articles the *objectiones* are devoted to anomalies, precepts which seem to violate the principle of explanation stated in the *corpus*. These *objectiones* are often numerous,[6] and in answering them Aquinas goes far beyond his usual pithy paragraph; the thousand-word response to the ninth objection in *Summa Theologiae Prima Secundae* 105.2 is not atypical. In effect, Aquinas inserted into the *Summa* a detailed commentary on the Mosaic Law. Perhaps as a result, the "Treatise on the Old Law" is undoubtedly the least read part of the *Summa Theologiae*; generations of students with no special interest in the topic have simply skipped ahead to the questions on grace and the *lex evangelica*.[7]

Several factors led Aquinas to abandon his customary brevity. Most important, perhaps, was the sheer complexity of the Law, which in itself would have made summary treatment difficult. But Thomas also had several axes to grind. For one, there was an exemplar he wanted to improve on: the treatise on law composed in the 1230s by the Franciscan John of La

Rochelle, which was included in a collaborative *Summa Theologica* attributed to Alexander of Hales.[8] In broad outline, Aquinas's treatment of law, proceeding from an analysis of law in general to natural law, human law, and finally divine law, follows John of La Rochelle, whom he clearly had read, but Aquinas made many improvements: his treatise is clearer, better organized, and more consistent.[9] Aquinas also felt compelled to integrate the moral commandments of the Pentateuch into the theory of natural law he had developed in Question 94. He went to considerable lengths to accomplish this, and the section on the moral precepts (Q. 100) is as important for understanding Aquinas's theory of natural law as it is for his ideas on the Mosaic Law and the Jews. In his "Treatise on the Old Law," Thomas was also responding to the challenge of Moses Maimonides' *Guide of the Perplexed*. In the *Guide*, which was translated into Latin sometime in the mid-1220s, Aquinas was confronted with a systematic attempt by a Jewish exegete to prove the Mosaic commandments could be understood as rational without positing Christ as their end. His treatment of the ritual precepts in particular is largely a response to Maimonides' work. Finally, Thomas's interpretation of the Law was influenced by yet another work: Aristotle's *Politics*, which was translated by William of Moerbeke in 1263, just a few years before Aquinas began the *Summa*. Thomas believed that by analyzing the "judicial" precepts (*iudicialia*) in terms of Aristotelian political categories he could prove that the Mosaic Law had established a uniquely just constitution or polity. This section of the "Treatise on the Old Law" shows Thomas at his best, bringing new ideas to bear on traditional problems, but it also adds considerably to the length of his treatise.

To a modern reader, Aquinas's treatment of the Mosaic Law appears highly anachronistic. Certainly his determination to divide and classify the Law produced some curious results: He transforms Moses into a philosopher-king, reads sophisticated political concepts and Roman legal ideas into a primitive tribal law, and uncritically repeats fanciful typological interpretations. But his analysis is not entirely naive. Thomas had learned from Aristotle that a wise legislator frames laws according to the specific needs of the citizens, and he had no doubt that God had carefully designed the Mosaic Law to meet the requirements of his chosen people. Unlike his patristic predecessors, he was not content simply to comb the Law in search of "types" of Christ; he also made a serious, if unavoidably speculative, effort to link what he called the "literal sense" of the Law's precepts to the historical context.

Lacking the resources of historical criticism and archaeology, Aquinas used what he had—the Bible itself, Maimonides' *Guide*, the Christian exegetical tradition, and sheer guesswork—to help him uncover the historical and social realities of the early Israelite community which could help explain the commandments. His starting point, drawn from his reading of the Pentateuch, was the thesis that the early Jews were a sorry lot, sorely in need of correction and guidance. At the time of the revelations to Moses at Sinai, the chosen people were cruel, avaricious, and prone to idol worship. A body of law that would prepare this people for the coming of the Messiah had to forbid idolatry, demand worship of the one true God, and inculcate moral virtue. But if God required too much too soon, the Jews would reject the Law out of hand. Because of this, Aquinas concluded, God designed the Law as a pedagogy that would immediately eliminate the worst religious and moral abuses while gradually teaching the Jews to aspire to higher forms of worship and behavior.

This pedagogy was designed to meet the needs of individuals as well as of the entire society. Thomas did not regard the Israelites as a monolithic group. His analysis is schematic, but he did recognize different levels of intelligence and natural inclination among the early Jews. Specifically, he distinguished three personality types—the "obstinate," the "ordinary," and the "excellent"—which he believed existed at all times among all peoples.[10] In revealing the Law, Aquinas believed, God took into account the specific requirements of these various groups.

> For the obstinate, the Law was given as a whip. The moral precepts were enforced through fear of punishment, and the ritual commandments were multiplied to prevent them from worshipping idols.
>
> For the proficient who are called "ordinary," the Law was a pedagogue: from the ritual commandments they learned how to truly worship God, while the moral precepts encouraged them to be just.
>
> For the perfect, the ritual commandments functioned as mystical signs, while the moral precepts assured them that their actions were upright.[11]

But there is a fundamental tension in Aquinas's analysis of the Law. At times, as in this passage, he speaks of the Law as a mechanism designed to inculcate virtue and true religion. Elsewhere, however, he portrays the Law as fundamentally impotent, incapable of producing righteousness. In this view, the revelation to Moses followed the long period of human history between the Fall and the Exodus, an era which had taught men that they were unable to grasp the moral law by their own power of reason. The Law that followed was a "pedagogy" only in that it taught men their will was impotent.

> [After the Fall] man prided himself on two things: namely his knowledge and his power. Regarding his knowledge, he believed that his natural reason could enable him to achieve salvation . . . and by experience he learned that his reason was defective as he sank to idol worship and the most degrading vices. . . . And after this time it was necessary to give a written law to remedy human ignorance. . . . But after man was instructed by the Law, his pride was convicted of weakness when he was unable to do what he knew was right.[12]

Thus conceived, the Law was intended to "convict men of their sins, not remit them."[13] By teaching men what was right without giving them the power to do it, the Law increased their guilt, because it made them fully conscious that their actions were wrong.[14] Furthermore, by prohibiting wrongdoing, the Law actually increased the desire or inclination to sin. Aquinas analyzes this psychological process at length.

> People think little of what they have, but they regard things that are beyond them as greater or more desirable. Thus prohibiting something desirable puts it beyond their reach, but because it is forbidden, they want it more.
>
> Second, when feelings are suppressed they tend to grow, whereas if they are expressed they diminish. We see this clearly in the case of grief or anger. Hence when someone refrains from something out of fear of punishment, the repressed desire for it is inflamed.
>
> Third, when we are allowed to do something, the knowledge that we can do it whenever we want often leads us to pass up opportunities to do it. But when something is forbidden us, we know we cannot always do it. As a result, when an opportunity arises in circumstances in which we need not fear being punished, we are quick to take it.[15]

According to Aquinas's analysis, the precepts of the Law were rules that merely regulated outward behavior and were unable to root out the evil desires that cause sin. The Law repressed desire, but this repression only increased the concupiscence that leads to sin. Rather than prevent sin, the Law made things worse. It actually intensified the desire to commit the acts it forbade, and, by teaching man the moral law, it made his sins more culpable because they were committed knowingly. This dichotomous view of the Law reflects the basic tension which pervades all of Aquinas's thought: the problem of remaining faithful to biblical and Catholic Christianity while using rationalistic categories to analyze its teachings. In the case of the Mosaic Law, the traditional Christian doctrine was derived from Paul. Aquinas was committed to upholding Paul's teaching, but at the same time he was guided by a generally Aristotelian understanding of the function of law in human society and, more specifically, by the teachings of Moses Maimonides on the nature of the Mosaic Law. Thus when he is commenting on Paul, as in his *Lectures on Romans*, or when he compares the Old Law with the reign of grace in the Christian dispensation (*Summa Theologiae Prima Secundae* [hereinafter *ST* 1–2] 105), Thomas writes as an orthodox Paulinian, emphasizing the shortcomings of the Law and its role as a stumbling block. But when he is engaged in the detailed exegesis of the Law, it is a Jew, Rabbi Moses Maimonides, who is his principal guide.

In *The Guide of the Perplexed*, Maimonides attempted to prove that the Law was perfectly—and hence divinely—designed to eliminate idolatry, inculcate religious truth, and make men virtuous. In carrying out this project, Maimonides wrote both as a philosopher and as a historian. That is, he tried to demonstrate that the commandments were in accord with the conclusions of speculative and practical reason, while also showing how the specific precepts—especially cleanliness laws and laws regulating the Temple cult—were rooted in the needs of the people of Israel at the time the Law was given. His method was essentially scholastic: he stated the Law's general purposes, divided its commandments into various categories, and examined each category in detail, explaining the rational and historical basis of the various precepts.

Maimonides wrote *The Guide of the Perplexed* sometime in the 1190s. By the mid-1220s it had been translated into Latin. Almost immediately this difficult work of Jewish apologetics found an audience among Christian intellectuals, especially in Paris. William of Auvergne relied heavily on Maimonides in composing his *De Legibus* in the early 1230s. A decade later, John of La Rochelle also borrowed freely from "Rabbi Moyses" in his analysis of the Law.[16] Aquinas probably did not know William's work firsthand, but he had read Maimonides and John, and his work continued this tradition. Like his predecessors, he accepted the basic Maimonidean principle that all the Mosaic precepts were grounded in reason and history, and in developing this approach in his "Treatise on the Old Law" he made only occasional and incidental references to Paul's strictures on the Law's inadequacy. Either Thomas did not see the chasm between Maimonides' positive evaluation of the Law and Paul's radical critique, or he chose to ignore it.

But Aquinas did not swallow *The Guide of the Perplexed* whole. He was too partisan a Christian for that. Rather, his interpretation subordinates the Law to Christ, in two ways. First, while he accepted Maimonides' claim that the Law was designed to impart religious truth and moral virtue, he denied that these ends were sufficient. According to Thomas, they were simply the necessary preconditions for the coming of the Messiah, who would bring the fullness of redemption; only a people weaned from idolatry and instructed in religion and morals would be able to recognize and accept the Savior. Second, while in his detailed analysis of specific precepts he repeated and developed Maimonides' rationalistic interpretations, Aquinas also insisted on the validity of patristic-style Christological exegesis. His strategy was to combine Maimonides' rabbinic approach with the wisdom of the Christian tradition. He aimed at a synthetic interpretation which would show that each commandment had a symbolic as well as a literal/historical meaning, and that both meanings served as a *preparatio Christi*.

At the beginning of his "Treatise on the Old Law," Thomas posed what appears at first glance to be an odd question: Does the Old Law contain more than one precept?[17] What he had in mind were scriptural passages like Matthew 7.12—"Do unto others as you would have them do unto you; this is the whole of the Law and the prophets"—as well as the general principle that divine law, the *lex vetus* as well as the *lex evangelium* or law of Christ, had the single goal of reconciling God and man. Aquinas responded by saying that while divine law has a single end or purpose, the objects that must be oriented to that end are diverse: "All the precepts of the Old Law are one in the sense that they are related to a single end, but they are many according to the diversity of objects they order to that end."[18] This rather elliptical statement, it turns out, means two things. First, there are various objects that must be placed in right relation to God, such as human actions, intentions, and institutions. Second, while the incarnation, passion, and resurrection of Christ are the means God chose to attain the ultimate end—the reconciliation of sinful mankind with himself—certain proximate ends had to be accomplished before Christ's redemptive work could take place: the Jews had to be established as a people and provided with moral and religious instruction. Mosaic Law was designed to fulfill these preconditions.[19]

Aquinas divided the precepts of the Mosaic Law into three categories: *moralia*, *caeremonialia*, and *iudicialia*.[20] All, he argued, are in some sense derived from natural law. The *moralia*, in his view, are identical with natural law precepts. Though these commandments can in principle be grasped by unaided practical reason, God revealed them to confirm and make known to all Jews what otherwise would have been known only "by a few, after a long time, and with the addition of many errors."[21] The relationship of the *caeremonialia* and *iudicialia* to natural law is more complex. Natural law demands that God be honored and society be organized for the common good, but these requirements can be fulfilled in a variety of ways. In Aquinas's terminology, this process of specifying the requirements of natural law by choosing among a number of licit options is called *determinatio*. Before God revealed the Law, these religious and political *determinationes* were matters for human choice. Thus Abraham, unbound by any ritual law, spontaneously offered sacrifice to God.[22] But because the Jews were the chosen people, destined to fulfill a unique role in salvation history, God himself specified their religious and political duties. He gave the people of Israel the *caeremonialia* to inculcate true knowledge of him, insure they would offer acceptable worship, and symbolically prefigure Christ,[23] and he designed the *iudicialia* to create a uniquely just political society.[24]

For Aquinas, the *moralia* are central. Not only are *caeremonialia* and *iudicialia* derived from them, since they specify the general duties to honor God and treat other humans with justice, but these moral commandments also provide an important link between the Old and New Testaments. Because they are in fact natural law principles, the *moralia*, and in particular the Ten Commandments, were not abrogated by Christ. According to Thomas, there is a direct link between these precepts and the legitimate ends of any body of law: justice, virtue, and the common good. As a result, no one, not even God, could rightly enact laws contrary to the Ten Commandments.

> For the precepts of the first tablet, which orient man toward God, are intrinsically and necessarily related to the general and final good of human life, which is God. The precepts of the second tablet, however, are intrinsically related to justice in human society; namely, they command that no one do what is unjust, and to give to each his due. In this manner the rational basis of the precepts of the Decalogue should be understood, and it is for this reason that they are completely indispensable.[25]

Christ's moral teaching deepened his followers' understanding of the *moralia*, and Jesus also provided counsels which made it easier to live an upright life, but he did not invalidate or change the moral teaching of the Mosaic Law.[26] Aquinas argued that while the rest of the Mosaic Law is related to Christianity as potency is to act, or image to reality, the *moralia* provide a thread of unbroken continuity.[27]

Because Aquinas identified *moralia* with natural law, it is important to discuss his conception of the *lex naturalis*. As noted, he identified natural law with rational morality, the knowledge of right and wrong attainable by the human mind. He believed that natural law forms the subject matter of a practical science whose deductive structure is analogous to that of the speculative sciences; morality, in Aquinas's theory, proceeds from self-evident axioms to general laws which are applied to specific cases.[28] The first principle of all practical reason is "good is to be done and pursued, and evil avoided."[29] Though natural law presupposes it, this principle is not specifically moral; it is as important for carpentry and shipbuilding as for ethics. Nevertheless, it does provide the foundation of Aquinas's entire natural law theory, for it demands that all moral precepts be related to the proper good of human beings, namely happiness or flourishing in the fullest sense.

Thomistic natural law is a three-tiered structure.[30] At its base are very general, easily grasped principles: humans should love God and neighbor, preserve life and reproduce it, seek knowledge and avoid ignorance.[31] Aquinas believed that every adult of minimal intelligence knows these principles are true.[32] The second level of natural law consists of more specific principles: do not lie, do not steal, honor your father and mother. Thomas thought that virtually everyone understands and accepts these principles as well, but noted there could be exceptions: "Occasionally human judgment may be perverted concerning these principles, so that they need to be promulgated."[33] In extreme cases, he argued, entire cultures can be ignorant of one or more of these commandments.[34] The third level of natural law consists of specific principles that are arrived at through *determinationes*—prudential decisions—made in light of more basic axioms. These principles are not and cannot be known by all. Only the wise are able to grasp them, and they must teach others, especially the young.

At first sight, Aquinas's explanation of the relation of *moralia* to natural law appears straightforward. He claims that the Ten Commandments are identical with the second level of natural law precepts, while the other moral commandments of the Mosaic Law constitute part of natural law's third, most obscure tier.

> Some commandments are more specific . . . and these are the precepts of the Decalogue. There are others however whose rational basis is not clear to everyone, but only to the wise, and these are the moral precepts that were added (*superaddita*) to the Decalogue, given to the people by God through Moses and Aaron.[35]

Thomas's account of the second "tablet" of the Decalogue (the fourth through tenth commandments), which contains precepts governing human relations, is consistent with this analysis. Arguing that these precepts correspond with the second tier of natural law principles, he goes on to show how more specific precepts are related to them. Thus he links prohibitions of hatred and violence with the commandment that forbids killing, argues that the precepts condemning fornication and homosexuality are based on the principle embodied in the commandment against adultery, and so on.[36]

But with the first tablet of the Decalogue (commandments one through three), matters are more complex. According to Aquinas, practical reason demands that man pay homage to God and avoid idolatry. These duties are the moral foundation for the first three commandments. As such they are second-level natural law precepts. The content of these commandments, however, is not limited to such broad principles. The third commandment, for example—"Remember the Sabbath and keep it holy"—is much more specific. In fact, it is not really a moral commandment at all. A precept demanding that *some* day be set aside for worship might qualify as a third-level natural law precept, but a commandment specifying the precise day for such devotion could never be arrived at via pure practical reason. Aquinas relies on a distinction to account for this.

> The commandment to observe the Sabbath is, in a sense, moral, in that it instructs man to reserve some time for worship. . . . It is under this description that it is counted among the commandments of the Decalogue. The specification of a particular time of worship is not, properly speaking, part of the Decalogue, because in this sense the commandment is ceremonial.[37]

Thomas is forced to make further distinctions with the commandments "Do not make a likeness or graven image" and "Do not take the Lord's name in vain." Interestingly, he does not include them among the *caeremonialia*, but instead claims they are sui generis, part of a level of precepts which are related in some unspecified way to natural law but which can be known only via revelation.[38]

Aquinas was not breaking new ground when he identified *moralia* with natural law and argued that the Gospel did not abrogate this portion of the Mosaic Law. This position had become orthodoxy a millennium before, in the aftermath of the second- and third-century struggles with the Manicheans and Antinomians. What is original in Thomas's account is the sophistication of his natural law theory and the ingenious way he integrated the *moralia* into it. Also, there is a marked contrast between his highly positive attitude toward the moral teaching of the *lex vetus* and that of some of his contemporaries, especially the Franciscans, who were more inclined to stress the Old Law's inadequacies and emphasize the originality of Jesus' ethical doctrine.

As impressive as his treatment of the *moralia* is, however, Aquinas is ultimately incoherent on the question of the historical efficacy of these precepts. As noted, he believed the moral commandments were intended to enable the people of Israel to judge more certainly between right and wrong. Why was this important? To make friendship between God and the Jews possible, he answered.

> The divine law is intended primarily to bring man into friendship with God. But since similarity is the basis of love . . . it would be impossible for there to be friendship from man to God, who is supremely good, unless man was made good. . . . Hence it was necessary for the Old Law to prescribe virtuous actions. These precepts are the moral commandments.[39]

It is difficult to reconcile this response with the Pauline doctrine that the Law was a stumbling block that actually increased sin and thereby proved conclusively that man cannot attain righteousness by his own efforts. Aquinas recognized this tension, at least in part. In the same article he posed an objection: How can the moral commandments be good, if they are part of a law Paul called the *littera occidens*? Thomas appeals to Augustine in his reply.

> As Augustine proves in his book *On the Spirit and the Letter*, in the case of the moral precepts, the letter of the Law is said to kill by providing an occasion for sin; that is, it prescribes what is good without providing the grace needed to do it.[40]

But this reply elides the principal question: Did the Law in fact make the Jews a uniquely virtuous people worthy of God's friendship, or did it lead them into sin? Aquinas wants to have it both ways. Torn between his loyalty to Paul and his Aristotelian belief in the efficacy of practical reason and the virtues, Thomas raises the discussion to a purely abstract level—the predisposition to justice versus justice itself, justification with God versus performing just acts—and manages to avoid entirely the question of the Law's effectiveness in making Israel a holy people.[41]

Similar ambiguities plague Aquinas's analysis of the *caeremonialia*. In his account, these commandments specify the general duty to worship and revere God mandated by natural law, a duty that must be fulfilled by exterior as well as interior observances. "Man is oriented toward God not only through the interior mental acts, which are to believe, to hope, and to love, but also through certain outward works by means of which he offers divine service."[42] For Aquinas, however, the *caeremonialia* do more than specify how man should show reverence to God. Like the moral commandments, they have a pedagogical function: they are designed to root out idolatry and inculcate a true understanding of God. Furthermore, the ceremonial precepts are also prophetic. They are *figurae*, anticipatory symbols of Christ, the Church, and heaven.

> The rational basis of the ceremonial precepts of the Old Law can be understood in two ways. One way is by considering the nature of the divine cult as it was then practiced. This is the literal meaning of the precepts. Understood in this way, the commandments were designed to prohibit the worship of idols, or commemorate blessings received from God, or to indicate some divine excellence, or to produce the mental disposition that was then required for worshipping God. Another way to explain these commandments is to show how they prefigured Christ. These explanations are symbolic and mystical. Understood in this way, the commandments may be taken to symbolize Christ and his Church, which is the allegorical meaning; or Christian morals, which is the moral meaning; or the state of heavenly glory to which Christ will lead us, which is the anagogical meaning.[43]

In other words, Aquinas believed the commandments should be understood according to the four "senses" of traditional Christian biblical exegesis: literal, allegorical, moral, and anagogical. Acutely aware of Maimonides' efforts in *The Guide of the Perplexed* to show that all the Mosaic commandments could be understood on the purely hstorical/literal plane, Thomas was careful to insist on the need for symbolic interpretation as well as literal exegesis. At one point, he refers to Maimonides' claim that some ceremonial precepts had no clear rational basis.[44] Aquinas agrees, noting that symbols are inherently obscure.

> The explanation of the ceremonial commandments is in a certain sense probable. They are not called "ceremonial" because their rational basis is unclear, however; rather, they are obscure because of their nature . . . for all precepts relating to the worship of God are necessarily symbolic . . . and this is why their rational basis is not entirely clear.[45]

Aquinas's basic point here is that all external worship symbolizes or expresses an interior disposition toward God. In fact, to be symbolic of, or ordered to, something else is characteristic of the *caeremonialia*, in contrast with the moral commandments, which are per se rational.[46] But to understand a symbol is to know what it symbolizes. And according to Thomas the cultic precepts of the Law were meant to symbolize Christ as well as the interior disposition of the worshipper; in fact, he argues elsewhere that this was their *primary* meaning—the fact that they were also a means for Jews to express their devotion to God was merely secondary.[47] Interpreters must supplement literal exegesis with typology if they hope to grasp the full significance of the *caeremonialia*.

To demonstrate the method he recommended, Aquinas carried out a detailed analysis of the *caeremonialia* in his "Treatise on the Old Law," noting both the literal/historical and symbolic meaning of dozens of commandments. To reduce the vast amount of ceremonial material in the Law to more managable proportions, he divided it into four broad categories, using his understanding of the nature of *cultus* as the principle of division. As Thomas defines it, cult consists primarily of the act of worship itself, but it also includes the various preconditions that make acceptable worship possible. Sacrifice is the primary act of worship, at least under the Mosaic Law, so it constitutes the major category. The other ceremonial precepts are divided into three sub-categories based on how they are related to sacrifice. *Sacra*, "sacred things," includes the Temple, the altar and other physical instruments of sacrifice, and festivals such as Passover and the Feast of Tabernacles. The *sacramenta* are the various purification rites that prepare the priests and people for worship; as the name indicates, Thomas thought many of them prefigured various elements of the Catholic sacramental system. The final category, *observantiae*, consists primarily of dietary regulations.[48]

From here Aquinas proceeds to the specific exegesis of the various types of *caeremonialia*. His method is to state an interpretive principle in the body of the article, then deal with specific examples in the *objectiones*. The process is lengthy and often tedious; fortunately an overview of Aquinas's approach will be sufficient for our purposes.

Broadly speaking, Thomas thought the literal or historical purpose of the commandments related to sacrifice was to emphasize man's dependence on God and discourage idolatrous practices, while the precepts governing sacred instruments, holy days, purification rituals, and pious practices (such as dietary regulations) were designed to inculcate doctrinal truths, instill a sense of awe and reverence toward God, and keep alive the memory of God's saving deeds. In addition, each type of commandment had a typological meaning. *Sacrificia* foretold the passion and death of Christ. *Sacra* represented the mysteries of Christ and his Church as well as Christian holy days. *Sacramenta* prefigured the Christian sacraments. Finally, *observantiae* symbolized the virtues and vices of the Church's moral taxonomy.[49]

Aquinas applies these principles to specific commandments in his replies to the objections. In the "Treatise on the Old Law," two basic types of objection are brought to bear against the cultic precepts: prophetic criticisms of the Temple cult and objections that a specific act prescribed by the Law is unfit or inappropriate for the worship of God. Thomas disposes of the former via a distinction; the prophets, he claims repeatedly, only criticized insincere worship, and did not mean to condemn the cult as such. He rebuts the second type of objection by arguing that typological *and* literal/historical reasons can be found for all the commandments, even those that seem completely irrational or arbitrary. By adopting the position that each and every commandment was grounded in the historical needs of the Jewish people, and that none had purely symbolic significance, Aquinas consciously chose to follow Maimonides rather than the patristic tradition. On the other hand, he is always careful to insist that each commandment also has a typological meaning. His treatment of the commandment "Do not boil a kid in its mother's milk" (Ex. 23.19) provides an interesting example of his approach.

> Although the dead kid does not feel any pain when it is cooked, it still seems somewhat cruel to use milk, which was intended for its nourishment, to cook its flesh. Or it may be that the pagans cooked the flesh of a kid in this way in their idolatrous worship, as a sacrifice or holocaust . . .
>
> Symbolically, this prohibition prefigures the fact that Christ, who was a "kid" because of his "likeness to sinful flesh" (Rm. 8.3), was not "cooked" by the Jews—that is, they did not kill him—in "his mother's milk," i.e. when he was an infant. Or it means that a "kid," or sinner, should not be "cooked in his mother's milk," that is, he should not be praised or flattered.[50]

Most patristic writers—including Augustine—believed that this commandment was irrational and was prescribed simply to test the obedience of the Jews.[51] Aquinas disagreed; he argued the commandment was meant to discourage cruelty, and he also followed Maimonides in suggesting that it may have been directed against a pagan practice. But he supplemented his historical interpretation with traditional, prefigurative exegesis. This combination of a speculative, Maimonidean attempt to understand the historical context of the ceremonial commandments with fanciful symbolic interpretation is typical of his approach to the Old Law.

Thomas used a similar strategy in approaching the theologically more significant issue of circumcision. In response to an objection that argued that ritual shedding of human blood smacked of paganism, Aquinas defended circumcision on historical, rational, and symbolic grounds.

> The literal reason for circumcision was to proclaim faith in the unity of God. And because Abraham was the first to be separated from the unbelievers . . . he was the first to accept circumcision. . . . In order that this proclamation and imitation of the faith of Abraham might be firmly established in the hearts of the Jews, they accepted a physical sign which could not be forgotten. . . . The eighth day was prescribed [for circumcision] because before this a boy is very delicate and might be hurt. . . . It was not delayed longer so that people should not fail to perform the operation out of sadness, and so that the parents, whose affection for the child grows as they care for it and spend time with it, should not refuse to allow it. A second literal reason is that the operation diminishes sexual desire. A third reason was to eliminate worship of Venus and Priapus, for whose sake that part of the body was revered . . .
>
> The symbolic explanation of this commandment is that it prefigured the removal of physical corruption by Christ, which will be perfectly completed in the eighth age, which is the age of resurrection.[52]

In its literal sense, Aquinas defends circumcision as a pedagogy, an outward sign which would remind Jews of their obligation to be faithful to the God of Abraham. He also buttresses this argument with other considerations: following Maimonides, he claims that circumcision inhibits sexual desire,[53] and, in a curiously anachronistic interpretation, Aquinas says it was also designed to discourage devotion to Venus and Priapus, the Greco-Roman gods of sexual love. (Presumably he knew the Canaanites worshipped similar deities.) On symbolic grounds, Thomas sees circumcision as prefiguring the triumph over physical corruption accomplished by Christ. He even provides a literal and symbolic explanation for why circumcision was performed on the eighth day: If the operation was performed earlier, it would be dangerous to the infant, while beyond that age their growing affection for the child might make the parents reluctant to allow it. Aquinas also borrowed this line of thought from Maimonides.[54] Anagogically, circumcision represents the perfect triumph over corruption that will occur at the time of the general resurrection—the eighth age of human history in the Augustinian scheme.

Underlying Aquinas's analysis of the *caeremonialia* is an approach to the Bible at once quintessentially medieval and strikingly innovative. For the medieval theologian, *everything* was significant, because the world is God's handiwork; it is designed according to a rational plan and is suffused with meaningful signs. This holds true above all of the Bible, for it is here that God expressed himself in words and concepts. In interpreting the

Old Testament, and especially the Mosaic Law, patristic and early medieval exegetes were obsessed with finding parallels and foreshadowings to link the outmoded precepts of the Old Law with Christ and his Church. All that was required to prove the Mosaic commandments rational was to find some point of similarity between the precept and Christian dogma. Animal sacrifice foreshadowed the Crucifixion, because in each case blood and death were involved; every mention of water was a "type" of Christian baptism; laws prescribing ritual cleanliness were said to symbolize precepts of Christian morality since both involved "purity," albeit of different kinds. This drive to note such parallels, so foreign to modern thought, continued to be important to thirteenth-century thinkers such as Aquinas. Typology was no longer cutting edge, and exegetes were largely content to repeat what others had said, but the presuppositions underlying symbolic interpretation were too deeply rooted for it to be jettisoned entirely. As J. Huizinga wrote:

> [Symbolism] supplied a very earnest craving of the medieval mind. . . . Symbolist thought permits of an infinity of relations between things. Each thing may denote a number of distinct ideas by its different special qualities, and a quality may also have several symbolic meanings. The highest conceptions have symbols by the thousand. Nothing is too humble to represent and to glorify the sublime. The walnut signifies Christ; the sweet kernel is his divine nature, the green and pulpy outer peel is his humanity, the wooden shell between is the cross. Thus all things raise the thoughts to the eternal; being thought of as symbols of the highest, in a constant gradation, they are all transfused by the glory of divine majesty.[55]

But while typology played an important role in Aquinas's interpretation of Old Testament *caeremonialia*, he approached the biblical text with a broader conception of what it meant for scripture to be rational. For him, it was not enough to link an Old Testament passage with its New Testament parallel. To show that the Law was fully rational, each commandment had to be justified on historical and philosophical grounds as well. Of each precept, Thomas sought to answer three questions: How does it prefigure Christ? How did it meet the needs of the people of Israel at that time and place? And, how is this precept related to rational morality, or natural law?

The juxtaposition of these questions gives his analysis of the *caeremonialia* its Janus-like quality of being simultaneously innovative and deeply traditional.[56] For Aquinas, however, the symbolic, historical, and rational meanings of the ritual precepts are not entirely disparate. In particular, the symbolism of the *caeremonialia* is central to his view of sacred history, for the symbolic meaning of these precepts do not simply foreshadow Christ; they also provide a tangible link between the faith of Old Testament Jews and that of Christians. This becomes clear in the course of Aquinas's response to a standard scholastic query: Did the *caeremonialia* impart saving grace to those who observed them? No, he replies, but in some cases their worship was an outward expression of an interior, saving faith in Christ.

> Because the mystery of the incarnation and passion of Christ had not yet truly been accomplished, the ritual precepts of that Law were not able in themselves to provide the grace flowing from the incarnation and passion, as the sacraments of the New Law do. . . . It was possible, however, for the mind of the faithful, at the time of the Law, to be joined by faith to Christ's incarnation and passion. In this way they were justified by their faith in Christ. The ceremonial precepts were able to manifest this faith, *in so far as these precepts were symbolic of Christ*. Similarly, sacrifices for sin were performed under the Old Law, not that they remitted sin, but they were a proclamation of the faith through which sins are forgiven. (Emphasis added)[57]

Aquinas makes several things clear in this passage. First, unlike the Christian sacraments, the *caeremonialia* do not per se confer grace. Second, even before the Incarnation it was possible to have a saving faith in Christ. Finally, it is precisely the symbolic meaning of the ritual precepts—"inquantum erant figura Christi"—that made it possible for them to be an expression of this faith.

This text, and others like it, also commits Aquinas to the position that some Jews, prior to the Incarnation, had an explicit faith in Christ and his saving work, and that for them the ritual commandments served primarily as a means of expressing that faith. In other words, some Old Testament Jews understood the *caeremonialia* in more or less the same way that Christian exegetes did. At one point Thomas declares that the only difference between Christians and the patriarchs of the Old Testament is that Christians believe Christ *has* come, whereas the patriarchs believed Christ *would* come.[58] In his view, typology is not merely the after-the-fact discovery of parallels between the Old and New Testaments. Rather, it was integral to the way Moses and his contemporaries understood the commandments.[59]

But Aquinas believed that only an elite group of Jews had explicit faith in Christ, or a detailed understanding of the prefigurative meanings of the *caeremonialia*. These were the wise men, the *perfecti*, of his threefold sociological scheme. Before Moses, only the patriarchs possessed this faith. After the Law was revealed, it was primarily the Levitical priests who were the *perfecti*.[60] The "obstinate" Jews, those especially inclined to sin, had no inkling of the Law's prefigurative sense; for them the *caeremonialia* served only to discourage idolatry. Nor did the *mediocres* have this kind of insight. They believed the Messiah would come, and they knew the ceremonial commandments somehow prophesied him, but that was all. Not until after Christ did it become possible for the ordinary believer to understand the mystical meanings of the *caeremonialia*.[61]

Aquinas's analysis of the ritual precepts is an astonishing tour de force. Rising to the challenge posed by Maimonides, Thomas beats the rabbi at his own game, supplementing his historical explanations and showing in detail how the commandments were tailored to the needs of the *duri*, the *mediocres*, and the *perfecti*, while at the same time insisting on the need for a Christocentric perspective if the Law's full meaning is to be grasped. His interpretation of the mystical sense of the ritual commandments makes it possible for him to insist that salvation can be attained only through an explicit faith in Christ while retaining the traditional Christian belief that the heros of the Old Testament were among the elect. "Though there were many *perfecti* and saints [before Christ], they were not saved through the works of the Old Law . . . [for] without the sacraments of the New Law there is no salvation."[62]

But this harmony between the Old and New Testaments is purchased at a price. Aquinas's typological scheme, like most allegorical interpretations of the Bible, is characterized by arbitrary and simplistic associations: honey symbolizes spiritual sweetness; salt incorruptibility; a dove charity and simplicity. Water invariably prefigures baptism; wine represents Christ's blood; every mention of wood is a reference to the Cross. In the "Treatise on the Old Law," symbolic association has no limits except those of Thomas's imagination, or rather the imaginations of the patristic and early medieval exegetes whose views were incorporated into the *Glossa ordinaria*, the standard medieval Bible commentary that was the source of most of Aquinas's imagery. There is no need to import "modern" or skeptical presuppositions to notice the arbitrary character of such typological interpretation; as early as the twelfth century some biblical scholars were critical of uncontrolled symbolic exegesis.[63] Aquinas's position also requires imagining Jews, hundreds of years before Christ, engaged in precisely this kind of typological analysis. The fact that he defended such a view even as he was attempting to find rational and historical grounds for the ritual precepts is a powerful reminder of how conservative a thinker Aquinas was. We shall have other occasions to note this conservative bent.

The three sections of the "Treatise on the Old Law" display a similar pattern: In each case Aquinas uses a rationalist theory or set of assumptions to frame his interpretation of the Pentateuch. Thus he examines the *moralia* in light of natural law doctrine; his treatment of the *caeremonialia* is guided by the presumption that all legislation must be grounded in historical and philosophical considerations; and he analyzes the *iudicialia* in terms of political categories and notions of distributive and retributive justice drawn from Aristotle. In isolating the "judicial" precepts for special analysis, Aquinas followed John of La Rochelle, who had done the same thing thirty years before in his treatise on the Mosaic Law.[64] But when John wrote, Aristotle's *Politics* had not yet been translated. Access to this work enabled Thomas to see the *iudicialia* as a polity as well as a civil and criminal code, something John, like Maimonides, had been unable or unwilling to do.[65] This interpretation helped focus the notion that the Mosaic Law had constituted the Jews as a *populus*. As Aquinas saw it, the Law did not simply provide the people of Israel with a body of moral precepts, liturgical instructions, and civil and criminal laws; it also gave them the political institutions they needed to implement these statutes and to modify them as circumstances demanded. The judicial precepts made it possible for the Law to become a *paideia*, capable of shaping character and inculcating values.

Aquinas believed the primary function of the Mosaic *iudicialia* was to order human relations. In this sense these precepts were similar to statute law. Their excellence derived from the way they transcended the minimal requirements for establishing peace and justice. Four- and even fivefold restitution for theft is called for to emphasize the gravity of the crime. Farmers are instructed to allow the poor to enter groves and eat what they like from fruit trees, and they are forbidden to glean their fields—what the harvesters miss should be left for the poor and the sojourner. Such laws were designed to inculcate charity, especially for the poor and powerless.[66] Aquinas also believed that, given the historical context, the Mosaic laws related to war were actually humane, since they required annihilation of the enemy only when there was a profound danger that survivors would lead the Jews into idolatry.[67] The law emancipating Hebrew slaves every seven years was intended to remind the Jews that God had freed them from Egypt and brought them into a covenant relation with himself. "Because the children of Israel were liberated by the Lord from servitude, and through this brought into divine service, the Lord did not wish them to be slaves in perpetuity. . . . Thus, because they were not slaves absolutely, but only in a certain sense, they were set free at the end of the time."[68] In sum, the civil and criminal precepts of the *iudicialia* were designed to encourage moral virtue in the broadest sense, yet they were also tailored to the needs of the people of Israel at a specific stage in history.

Aquinas found much to admire in the polity established by the Mosaic Law. In his view, two things were required for a well-ordered political society.

> One is that everyone have some part in the government. In this way peace is preserved among the people, and they will love and preserve such a polity, as Aristotle says in the second book of the *Politics*. The other is that care be taken in choosing the type of rule or government established.[69]

Aquinas argued that the constitution of Israel fulfilled both these requirements by combining the best elements of monarchy, aristocracy, and democracy. The Law allowed the Jews to choose their leaders from among themselves. This helped bind all the people of Israel to their government through a sense of participation, allowed a meritocracy to develop, and helped avoid the corruption endemic to a hereditary monarchy or aristocracy. Furthermore, the supreme ruler, chosen for his preeminent virtue, governed with the assistance of elders notable for wisdom and integrity.

> Moses and his successors governed as a single ruler over all princes, which is a type of kingship. Seventy-two elders were also chosen according to their virtue, however . . . and this was aristocratic. But the polity was democratic in that the rulers were chosen from, and by, the people. . . . Hence it is clear that the form of government that the Law instituted was the best possible (*optima*).[70]

For Aquinas then, the constitution outlined in the *iudicalia* was ideal, and its penal code tempered justice with mercy while working to make Israel a virtuous people. Yet his views on the basic rationale and historical effectiveness of these precepts are less clear-cut. In Question 99 of the *prima secundae*, where Thomas explicitly states why God instituted the *moralia* and *caeremonialia*, he suddenly becomes vague when he comes to the *iudicialia*. He notes that political and legal *determinationes* of natural law are required to establish a political society, but he does not indicate why God provided the Jews with such specific legislation, yet left the Gentiles to make their own arrangements.[71] He skirts the issue again in an article on the *ratio* or rationale of the judicial precepts.[72] Oddly enough, he confronts the question of the historical efficacy of the *iudicalia* only when he turns to a discussion of their prefigurative meaning. Furthermore, the answer, when it finally comes, is decidedly ambivalent. "The Jewish people were chosen by God so that Christ might be born from among them. Because of this it was necessary that the entire state (*status*) of that people be prophetic and symbolic."[73] This passage indicates that it was necessary for the Jews to be a holy people, since the Messiah was to be a Jew. But Thomas does not explain how the *iudicialia* could make Israel holy.

It is easy to see why Aquinas was uneasy dealing with this question. Had he faced it directly, he would have been confronted with the fundamental tension between his belief in the efficacy of law and practical reason and his commitment to a view of Jewish history derived from scripture and the Church Fathers. Thomas enthusiastically agreed with Maimonides that the Mosaic Law was divine and therefore supremely reasonable, and when he brought his reading of Aristotle's *Politics* to the Pentateuch and discovered a political constitution and civil and criminal code there, he gave those aspects of the Law his approbation as well. From Aristotle and others, however, he had learned that good law is law that works. Just as the moral commandments were revealed to provide the Jews with a firm and comprehensive understanding of moral principles, so the *iudicialia* were instituted to make Israel a well-ordered society; they were established "to order the condition of that people according to justice and equity."[74] Given this logic, it seems to follow that since they were from God, these precepts must have been effective. But for a Christian theologian, this conclusion was problematic. The notion that the *iudicialia* had molded Israel into a virtuous people with a uniquely just political society was difficult to reconcile with the Pauline doctrine that the Law was a stumbling block. Certainly Aquinas subsumed the proximate purposes of the *iudicialia* under the larger end of the *preparatio Christi*, but this did nothing to solve the dilemma. The question remained: *How* did the *iudicialia* prepare the way for the Messiah? In the "Treatise on the Old Law," Aquinas simply avoided the issue by keeping the discussion abstract. In this way he was free to praise the *iudicialia* without having to consider their historical effectiveness.

In several of his Bible commentaries, Aquinas did discuss the historical development of the people of Israel in the period before Christ. But no single, coherent interpretation of Jewish history emerges from these texts. Rather, the same basic duality reappears. The closest Aquinas came to providing a synoptic view was in the early *Commentary on Isaiah*, which was probably written between 1249 and 1252, when he was studying under Albertus Magnus at Cologne.[75] Here Thomas divided Israelite history into periods according to the modes of sacrifice offered in divine worship.

> Four periods may be distinguished. The first was before the written Law and idolatry. Then God was pleased by the ancient sacrifices of the holy fathers, both because of their devotion and because of what their offerings symbolized.
>
> The second period was under the written Law. One reason for the sacrifices that were mandated then was to distinguish them from idolatrous worship, for it would not have been appropriate for the same sacrifices to have been offered to God as were used in giving honor to Satan. Also, sacrifices were mandated as a means of keeping the people from idolatry, to which they were prone. This is why no sacrificial precepts were given before the making of the golden calf . . .
>
> The third time was that of the Prophets. At this time, because of the sins of the people, God was not pleased by their offerings as such, but only by what those offerings signified. Thus, in a sense, God was offended rather than pleased by their sacrifices.
>
> The fourth period is the era of grace, when all such sacrifices have been abolished, because with the coming of the truth, prefigurative symbols come to an end.[76]

A fairly clear picture of Jewish history emerges from this passage. The era of the patriarchs—Abraham, Isaac, and Jacob—was a golden age in which God's chosen offered him acceptable, spontaneous sacrifices. The Law was given at a time when the people of Israel were prone to idolatry. Hence its ritual precepts were intended to discourage idol worship. The age of the Prophets—the period between the death of Moses and the birth of Christ—was one of increasing corruption; the people were generally sinful and their sacrifices were no longer pleasing to God. Finally, with Christ, animal sacrifice was abolished. In sum, Jewish history is a chronicle of decline. Patriarchal virtue yields to widespread idolatry and corruption; the Law is given as a corrective, but fails.

Other passages in Aquinas confirm this general impression. In his commentaries on Isaiah and Jeremiah, Aquinas took prophetic hyperbole as a literal description of the spiritual state of the Jews. Furthermore, he applied prophetic condemnations to Jews throughout the prophetic period and beyond. Thus Aquinas accuses Old Testament Jews of all manner of iniquity: they are proud, obstinate, malicious, hypocritical, and unjust; they fail to help the poor; their priests misinterpret the scriptures and promulgate bad statutes; and they routinely violate the precepts of the Mosaic Law, even failing to observe the Sabbath, the lightest obligation the Law imposed on them.[77] And the process is progressive; taking up an Augustinian theme, Thomas claims that by the time of Christ the Jews were more iniquitous than they had been during the Egyptian captivity.[78]

Elsewhere, however, Aquinas gives a very different view of Jewish history. In the *Commentary on Romans* he claims that the Jews alone of all peoples understood God's true, spiritual nature and refrained from idol worship. Moreover, their grasp of morality was also superior, thanks to the Law; Jews could not only distinguish between right and wrong, but between actions that were truly virtuous and those that were merely licit.[79] His description of the Jews of Jesus' time is hard to square with the notion of a steady decline: Aquinas portrays them as essentially faithful to the Mosaic commandments, and he nowhere accuses first-century Jews of idolatry; apparently the Law had successfully eliminated this vice.[80]

In sum, Aquinas tried to have it both ways. In certain contexts, he presented Jewish history as a story of progressive degeneration; in others, he claimed that the Law was a pedagogy that inculcated moral and religious knowledge and made it possible for the Jews to receive their Messiah.[81] Like his treatment of the Law, Aquinas's view of Jewish history is important because it displays a duality that we have seen before and that will appear again. In his typological exegesis of the *caeremonialia*, Thomas interpreted the faith of Hebrew patriarchs and prophets in a cavalier and profoundly ahistorical manner, ascribing explicitly Christian beliefs to men who lived a thousand years before Christ. In his discussion of the moral precepts and the *iudicialia*, he consistently sidestepped the question of the Law's effectiveness. And throughout his "Treatise on the Old Law," as well as in his analysis of Jewish history, there is an unacknowledged tension between one description of the Jews as holy and beloved of God, and another that depicts them as sinful and degraded. These elisions and ambiguities will provide the dominant theme for the rest of this book.

4. *Gravissimum Peccatum*: The Crucifixion of Christ and the Guilt of the Jews

Sanguis Christi expetitur ab eis usque hodie.
—*Super Evangelium Matthaei* 27.25

Like all medieval theologians, Aquinas believed the death of Christ meant the end of Judaism as a legitimate religion. Judaism had been designed by God to prefigure Christ and make it possible for people to recognize him as the Messiah; the entire history of the Jewish people had been a *praeparatio Christi*. Now the Crucifixion had lowered the curtain on this act of the sacred drama. Practices that had once been virtuous and salvific—circumcision, sacrifice, keeping the Sabbath—would henceforth be blasphemous and loathsome in the sight of God. In Christ, the Jews were offered a choice: accept the salvation offered by the Crucified One, or incur exile and spiritual death. Those Jews who put their faith in Jesus would be counted among the elect, the *verus Israel*; those who rejected him were condemned to homelessness and degradation in this life and damnation in the world to come.

But Aquinas could not completely sever the ties between Christian and Jew. For him, as for other medieval theologians, the Jews were infidels, dangerous unbelievers unworthy of toleration. Yet there was always Paul: Paul who had testified to the Jews' zeal for God and their primacy over the Gentiles; Paul, who had defended himself before the Sanhedrin by allying himself with the Pharisees, and who proclaimed that the rejection of the Jews was only temporary, that God still loved them and would save them in the end. Aquinas believed the participation of first-century Jews in Jesus' crucifixion was the defining act of Jewish history, and that henceforth all Jews were cursed, but Paul's authority made it impossible for him to adopt a wholly negative attitude toward the Jews who continued to exist in the

Christian era. Instead, he developed a position characterized by the same antinomies that shaped his view of Jewish history before Christ: the Jews as holy and sinful, rejected and beloved.

There is a wealth of material in Aquinas's writings pertaining to first-century Jews, their role in the crucifixion of Christ, and the guilt they incurred by their actions, but it is diffuse, scattered throughout the *Summa Theologiae* and various Bible commentaries. One approach to reconstructing Aquinas's thought would be to analyze these sources piecemeal, perhaps by placing them in chronological order and examining them one at a time. Fortunately, however, such a cumbersome process is not necessary, since Aquinas's most important writings on the Jews at the time of Christ—the third part of the *Summa Theologiae*, the *Lecturae* on John and Matthew, and the commentaries on Romans and Psalms—were all written in the period 1268–1273, while he was in Paris and Naples.[1] This means Thomas dealt with these issues repeatedly during his most mature and productive years as a writer and theologian. In these various works Aquinas develops and clarifies his ideas, but there are no fundamental changes in his position. For this reason I will take a synthetic approach, freely juxtaposing passages from various texts in an effort to reconstruct the totality of Aquinas's thought.

Aquinas's portrayal of first-century Jewish society was, of course, shaped primarily by the biblical text. The Gospels provided the basic information that he had to integrate and explain. Thomas learned from all four Gospels that Jesus was followed by a core of disciples who—with the exception of Judas Iscariot—remained faithful to the end, as well as by a larger crowd that eventually turned against him. He also knew from these texts that the Pharisees and priests saw Jesus' popularity as a threat to their power. They repeatedly tried to discredit and trick Jesus, and in the end conspired against him to secure his arrest and execution. The Gospel of John provided the additional information that the Pharisees, as well as the Jews as a whole, were divided over Jesus: most condemned him, but others suspected he was a good man and possibly a prophet or even the Messiah.

In his exegesis, Aquinas attempted to dovetail these facts with his conception of the history of the Jews and their understanding of the Mosaic Law. Given the tensions and elisions of that conception, this was no mean task. His view of history demanded that he portray the Jews as simultaneously corrupt in morals and religion yet somehow also prepared to receive the Messiah. Similarly, his theory of Jewish guilt forced him to argue that the Jews were well enough versed in scripture to recognize Jesus' claim to be their savior, but that, in the end, it was ignorance of those same scriptures that allowed the Jews to reject and crucify Jesus.

Aquinas divided first-century Jews into two basic groups. He used a variety of terms to refer to them, depending on the context: *majores* and *minores*, *principes* and *populus*, *sapientes* and *stulta*.[2] By *majores*, *principes*, and *sapientes*, he primarily meant the Pharisees, though he often included scribes, elders, and the Temple priests in this category as well.[3] The *majores* were a spiritual elite, versed in the scriptures and capable of understanding the Old Testament prophecies. As such, it was their duty to give instruction to the common people. The *minores*, by contrast, were largely ignorant. They had a vague knowledge of scripture and history, and many of them piously observed the Mosaic precepts and waited hopefully for the Messiah, but for instruction on the Law and scriptural interpretation they were wholly dependent on the Pharisees and priests.

Aquinas was of two minds concerning first-century Jews: he excoriated their stubbornness and infidelity, yet he also believed that they faithfully kept the dietary laws and obeyed the Mosaic proscription on loaning money at interest to other Jews.[4] And he was convinced that in the era before Christ, conversion to Judaism was the best hope of salvation for the pagan nations.[5] God had revealed himself to the Jews alone.

> The Jews, through the Law and the Prophets, had a true knowledge or understanding of God; that is, they did not believe he was corporeal, or in a determinate place. . . . Nor did the Jews worship idols. . . . Likewise, only the Jews possessed true knowledge of God.[6]

Furthermore, when Jesus began his public ministry, it was precisely their Judaism that made it possible for many Jews to accept him as Christ. According to Aquinas, they believed his claims to be the long-awaited Messiah precisely because the Law had prepared them to do so.[7] Logically, it would seem that the Pharisees would be most likely to believe in Jesus, since their knowledge of the scriptures should have made it easy for them to recognize the validity of his claim to be the Messiah. Aquinas thought that for Nicodemus and some other Pharisees, this was the case. "Because their opinion was closer to the truth, Nicodemus was easily converted to Christ."[8] But any number of New Testament passages forced him to acknowledge that most of Jesus' followers were drawn from the common people rather than the religious elite. Aquinas offered an ingenious explanation of Christ's decision to call only a handful of learned men.

> It is true that from the beginning the Lord did not choose the wise, the powerful, or the well-born, so that the power of faith would not be attributed to human wisdom or power . . . nevertheless, he wished from the beginning to convert a few of the wise and powerful to himself, so that his teaching should not be received only by the lowly and ignorant and thus held in contempt; otherwise the multitude might have concluded that the belief of the converts was due to their lowliness and ignorance rather than the virtue of the faith.[9]

As he usually does in explaining virtuous actions performed by Jews, Aquinas emphasizes causal agents other than the Jews themselves. In this case, he argues that while Judaism provided the context, it was ultimately divine providence—not their own choice—that led some Jews to accept him as the Messiah.

It was easy for Thomas to explain why some Jews chose to accept Jesus, and even the anomaly of Jesus drawing the bulk of his followers from the *mediocres* rather than the *sapientes* could be finessed by an appeal to God's causality. The fact that most Jews rejected Jesus posed a knottier problem, however: If Jesus' teaching and miracles demonstrated that he was the Messiah, how could his own people repudiate and kill him? As we have seen, this had been an urgent question for the early Church. But by the thirteenth century it had lost some of its bite, thanks to the development of the stereotypical image of the malevolent Jew. Aquinas's strategy was simple: he relied on a relatively benign portrait of first-century Judaism together with divine causality to explain why some Jews had accepted Jesus, then appealed to the stereotype when it came time to explain why most had not. This approach was so deeply rooted in traditional exegesis that Thomas was probably not even aware of the tensions it concealed.

Following the Church Fathers, he used the Old Testament to denounce those who had rejected Christ. With no regard for hyperbole or original context, he shifted the full brunt of prophetic denunciation to first-century Jews. Like their ancestors, he argued, the Jews of Jesus' day were faithless, ungrateful, and guilty of all manner of sin, especially those sins to which scripture claims the people of Israel were especially prone: avarice, cruelty, pride, and hardness of heart. Rather than imitating the personal virtue of men like Abraham and Moses, they took pride in mere genealogical descent and presumptuously assumed that God would bless and save them because of their ancestry.[10] Warming to his topic, Aquinas waxes poetic in describing their malice: "Frigidi a caritate diligendi, sed ardentes aviditate nocendi, ut accederent animo circumveniendi, et circumdarent comprimentes, animo persequendi."[11] Explaining the Crucifixion, he argued that the Jews had profited little from centuries of instruction in the Law and their special share in divine providence. According to Aquinas, their religious training and knowledge of scripture made it possible for them to at least suspect Jesus was the Messiah, but in the end their vicious moral disposition led them to reject and crucify him.

Though Thomas thought general Jewish blindness and hardheartedness went a long way toward explaining why first-century Jews refused to accept Jesus, he believed the Pharisees and the common people also had their own, more specific reasons for rejecting him. Given his sociological views, he had little difficulty understanding the actions of the *mediocres*. As an intellectual of noble birth, Aquinas thought little of the common run of mankind. The wise, the faithful, the elect—all were distinctly minority categories for him.[12] His disdain for the first-century Jewish masses stemmed more from an elitist contempt for uneducated rustics than from hostility to Jews as such. For him, the *mediocres* were ignorant of the Law; at best, they had a superficial understanding of its precepts. Sensation and emotion were dominant among them, as they always were among the common people. Thus they followed Jesus eagerly at first; he was the latest fad. But, he argues, their devotion was shallow because it was based on the miracles Jesus performed rather than on any real understanding of his religious and moral teaching.

> They believed when they saw the miracles that Christ did. But their faith was weak because it was inspired by signs rather than by doctrine . . . and they did not believe in Christ as God, but simply as a just man or a prophet.[13]

Thomas also believed that crowds tend to suspect the worst. In the case of Jesus, when the meaning of his teaching eluded them, they immediately accused him of being in league with Satan. "His words were beyond human understanding . . . [and because] it is the custom among the unlettered to believe that what they cannot understand is diabolical, they believed that Christ spoke as if possessed by a demon."[14] The mob's fickleness and shallow understanding of his message made it possible for them to turn against Jesus as quickly as they had rallied to him.

While Aquinas's account of the reaction of the common people to Jesus is based on a few simple notions about group psychology, his analysis of the Pharisees and other religious authorities is more complex. Doctrinally, he thought, the *majores* were on the right track. "The Pharisees were closer to us in their opinions, because they believed in a future resurrection, and said that spiritual creatures existed . . . [and] their opinion was more probable, and closer to the truth."[15] In this passage, as in others, Thomas reveals a certain empathy for the Pharisees. An even more revealing example occurs elsewhere in his *Lectures on John*. Here, after condemning the Pharisees for accusing Jesus of being a Samaritan, Aquinas goes on to explain that the charge had a certain logic.

> The Jews said this about Christ for two reasons. One, because the Jews hated the Samaritans, since when the ten tribes went into captivity, the Samaritans took their land. . . . And because Christ was arguing with the Jews, they thought he was a Samaritan and an enemy, etc. Another reason is that the Samaritans observe some Jewish rites, but not others. Hence when the Jews saw that Jesus observed the Law in some matters, while in others he mitigated its rigor, as in the case of the Sabbath, they called him a Samaritan.[16]

In similar fashion, Aquinas notes in his *Lectures on Matthew* that even in flogging Jesus and demanding his crucifixion, the Jewish leaders acted according to the Law; that is, the penalties imposed on Jesus were those prescribed by the Law for the crimes of which he was accused.[17] It may be that as a theologian, priest, and friar Thomas was conscious of an analogy between the Pharisees and the medieval clerical elite. Certainly his belief that virtue was largely monopolized by the educated class would have been consistent with a tendency to identify with the Jewish *sapientes*.

But this tendency, if it was such, was circumscribed by his ideas about sacred history. As noted above, Aquinas was convinced that Judaism had become corrupt during the Prophetic era and that the Mosaic ceremonial precepts had ceased to be pleasing to God. As a result, whereas he believed that earlier Jewish religious elites, such as the Levitical priests of Moses' day, had been proto-Christians who fully understood the prefigurative meanings of the Law, Aquinas was unwilling to make this claim on behalf of the Pharisees. An even stronger check on any pro-Pharasaic sentiment was provided by the utterly negative portrayal of Pharisees in the Gospels, particularly in Matthew and John, on which Aquinas wrote commentaries. Thomas read the Bible through the filter of his own ideas and prejudices, but in the end he was bound to the text. He praised the Pharisees for their doctrinal soundness and offered an occasional apology for their suspicions of Jesus, but he also reserved his harshest condemnations for the Jewish *principes*.

In excoriating the Pharisees, Aquinas was following an old tradition; taking their cue from Matthew 23, all patristic and medieval commentators felt obliged to attack the Pharisees in the harshest possible terms. If anything, Aquinas toned down the bitter invective that Origen, Jerome, and Chrysostom had made standard. But his analysis of the *malitia principiorum* is second to none in its dissection of the depth and variety of the sins committed by the priests and Pharisees, and the heated rhetoric of certain passages contrasts sharply with Aquinas's usually placid prose.

According to Aquinas, the chief sin of the Pharisees was pride. As revered leaders they had grown arrogant and jealous of their powers. One sign of this arrogance was the way they had perverted the Law. Thomas did not believe the Pharisees' practice of supplementing the written Law with human traditions was intrinsically sinful. He recognized this process as inevitable and even desirable; all law is framed in general terms and requires interpretation and *determinatio*.[18] In carrying out this legitimate task, however, the Pharisees had been guilty of cruelty and presumption: they had been cruel because they made the Law so rigorous that virtually no one could keep its precepts, and they were presumptuous in pretending their decisions had divine authority.[19] It was this same cruelty and presumption, flowing from pride, that led the Pharisees to reject Jesus.

In Aquinas's analysis, human actions can be immoral in a number of ways: either because they are intrinsically evil, or because they are done for the wrong reason, in the wrong way, or under the wrong circumstances.[20] The hostility of the *principes* to Jesus, he thought, was to be condemned on all these counts. Their opposition was intrinsically wrong: in rejecting the Messiah who had come to liberate mankind, they had allied themselves with Satan. The basic malice of this act was exacerbated by their intentions and methods and by the circumstances in which they acted. Aquinas believed the Pharisees and Temple priests were motivated by sheer self-interest. They saw Jesus' popularity as a threat to their own standing among the people, and they also feared the Romans might view Jesus as an agitator or revolutionary and destroy the Temple, or even all of Jerusalem, in retaliation, thus eliminating their base of power.[21] The Pharisees' efforts to discredit Jesus were completely unscrupulous: they slandered him, cloaked their attacks on him in the guise of zealotry, tried to trip him up with trick questions, and attempted to sow discord among his closest disciples. Finally, the fact that the Pharisees were doctors of the Law who should have recognized the truth of Jesus' claims also compounded the sinfulness of their actions.[22]

Aquinas's discussion of the role of the Jews in the death of Jesus ultimately revolves around two questions. The first is essentially historical: How could the Jews have killed the Messiah they had expected for centuries and whose coming was the culmination of their entire history as a people? The second is theological: How could Jesus' death, which brought about the salvation of the human race, cause the Jews to be condemned?

In large measure, the first question has already been answered. Aquinas believed that the same combination of Jewish hardheartedness, Pharasaic pride, and mob psychology which led the Jews to reject Jesus' claim to be their savior also inspired them to seek his execution. Still, Thomas had to deal with a puzzling anomaly. Jesus was God incarnate, and as such was omnipotent. It followed that the Jews could not have killed him had not Jesus—as well as God the Father—permitted them to do so; in fact, given that God is the ultimate cause of all things, he actually had to *want* the Jews to kill Jesus. But if this was true, how could the Jews be blamed for doing what God wanted them to do? Furthermore, the Jews had not actually killed Jesus themselves; a Roman governor, Pontius Pilate, gave the order of execution, and Roman soldiers drove home the nails. If there was blame to be laid, should not some of it be shared by others who played a role in Jesus' death?

This conundrum was sheer grist for scholastic analysis, calling for precisely the type of subtle distinctions in which medieval theologians excelled. In this case, the most important distinction was based on the principle that the morality of an action depends on the motive or intention of the agent. God willed the Crucifixion because it was salvific; Christ submitted to suffering and death out of obedience to the Father. Pontius Pilate, the soldiers, and the Jews, by contrast, had been parties to murder. This basic distinction, which is implicit in the New Testament itself, had been pointed out by all the Church Fathers, though the details of their analysis differed. The twelfth-century theologian Peter Lombard, whose *Sentences* became the standard manual of theology in medieval universities, provided the definitive scholastic formulation: God willed the Crucifixion for the sake of its effects, but he did not desire the sinful intentions of the Jews.

> We say that it should be conceded that God wanted Christ to suffer and die, since his suffering was good and was the cause of our salvation. But when we say "He wished him to suffer and die at the hands of the Jews," we must make a distinction. If this statement is taken to mean that God wanted him to undergo suffering and death, which was brought about by the Jews, then this is true. If however the statement is taken to mean that God wanted the Jews

> to kill him, this is false. For God did not will the action of the Jews, which was evil. Rather, he desired the good of Christ's suffering, and this wish was fulfilled through the evil desires of the Jews.[23]

Lombard's formulation got God off the hook and placed the blame for Jesus' death squarely on the Jews, but it did not deal with the other parties to the Crucifixion—Judas, Pilate, and the Roman soldiers. In the 1230s, Alexander of Hales tried to tie up these loose ends by analyzing the Crucifixion in causal terms. Alexander's approach pointed toward a solution, but a shaky grasp of Aristotelian concepts muddied his analysis.

> God the Father was the efficient cause of the death of Christ, in that he permitted it and did not prevent his death when he was able. Christ was the efficient cause, in that he voluntarily accepted death and did not prevent it, though he could have. Judas and the Jews, however, were the efficient cause as procuring agents, while those who actually crucified him were the efficient cause in the sense that they actually caused his death.[24]

Though suggestive, this passage is something of a hodge-podge. In Aristotelian terminology, the efficient cause is the agent that immediately produces an effect. For example, the action of hand, mallet, and chisel are the efficient causes of a sculpture. In ascribing efficient causality to God, who "participated" in Jesus' death only by not intervening to prevent it, Alexander makes the term "efficient cause" so elastic that it becomes almost meaningless; on his account, every passive spectator of an event is an efficient cause. This awkward use of Aristotle should not surprise us; the Philosopher's writings were still being translated in the 1230s, and the difficult work of appropriating his ideas was far from complete. It would be another generation before the circulation of Averroes' commentaries and the production of new Latin commentaries on Aristotle's writings by men such as Robert Grosseteste, Albert the Great, and Aquinas himself would create a standardized Aristotelian terminology.

Aquinas, writing almost forty years after Alexander, dealt more effectively with the problem. Like his Franciscan counterpart, he took Peter Lombard as his starting point: God willed the redemption effected by Christ's death, but he did not desire the sinful act that produced it.[25] But in sorting out the specific roles of the various agents, Thomas did not use the term "efficient cause" to describe the actions of Christ and God the Father. Christ, Aquinas argued, was the cause of his own death only in an indirect or passive sense, in the same way someone could be said to have flooded a room because he did not close the window before it rained.[26] God the Father "caused" Jesus' death in three ways: Christ's Passion was part of God's plan to liberate the human race; the Father inspired Christ with the love that made him willing to suffer for sinful men; and, like Jesus himself, God did not prevent Christ's death, though it was in his power to do so.

Having clarified the role played by God and Jesus in bringing about the Crucifixion, Aquinas turned to another issue: the motives, and hence the relative merit or guilt, of the various agents.

> The same action may be judged as good or evil in various ways, depending on its motives. The Father delivered Christ over to death out of love; hence he should be praised. Christ's own motive was the same. Judas, on the other hand, delivered Christ out of greed; the Jews out of envy; and Pilate out of the worldly fear that made him fear Caesar. Hence they should be condemned.[27]

Elsewhere, Thomas accounts for the soldiers' role as well: they were simply following orders.[28]

In this passage, Aquinas concentrates on the motives of the various agents rather than on causality as such. The emphasis is characteristic of his theory of human action. For Thomas, the search for Aristotelian causes is proper to physics or metaphysics, but in the realm of human acts it is intentionality, ends, means, and circumstances that count. It is this element of rationality and choice that makes human actions moral and hence deserving of reward or punishment.[29]

Aquinas's emphasis on the role of motivation also made it easier for him to deal with the question of Jewish guilt for the Crucifixion. As was shown earlier, the belief that all Jews—not just Jesus' contemporaries—were guilty of his death and deserved to be punished was an axiom of patristic and medieval thought. Along with the fear of Jews as a source of doctrinal contagion, it was a primary determinant of canon law and social policy in the Middle Ages. The *culpa Iudaeorum* was the foundation of everything from discriminatory legislation to the doctrine that the Jews were serfs of the Church or the state.

But the thesis that the Jews *in toto* were guilty for Jesus' death posed serious intellectual and exegetical problems. In the first place, the culpability of even first-century Jews was difficult to determine. No doubt the Gospels were clear on some points: the Jews of Jerusalem, urged on by their leaders, had goaded a reluctant Pilate into giving the order of execution. But there was strong biblical evidence that they had acted out of ignorance, unaware that they were crucifying the Messiah. Luke 23.34a, I Corinthians 2.8b, and Acts 3.17–18 all seemed to support this view.

> Father, forgive them: for they know not what they do.
>
> For if they had known it, they would never have crucified the Lord of Glory.
>
> And now, brethren, I know you did it through ignorance, as did your rulers (*principes*). But those things which God before had showed by the mouth of all the prophets, that his Christ should suffer, he has thus fulfilled.[30]

Taken at face value, these passages seem to absolve first-century Jews of guilt. The Jews may have killed an innocent man, but since they had not known he was Christ, they were not guilty of consciously slaying their Messiah, much less of deicide.

Other texts, however, lent themselves to a different interpretation. Christian exegetes saw the parable of the rebellious workers who killed the vineyard owner's son (Mt. 21.33–39; Mk. 12.1–8; Lk. 20.9–15) as a clear reference to the Jews' role in the Crucifixion. John 9.39–41 and 15.22–24 were even more damning.

> Jesus said: I have come into this world for judgment, that those who do not see may see, and those who see may become blind. Some of the Pharisees who were with him heard this and said to him: Are we also blind? Jesus said to them: If you were blind, you would not have sin. Now, however, you say "We see"; therefore your sin remains.
>
> If I had not come and spoken to them, they would not have sin; but now they do not have an excuse for their sin. He who hates me, also hates my father. If I had not done works among them such as no one has ever done, they would not have sin; now however they have seen and they hate both me and my father.

Taken together, these two sets of texts posed a difficult hermeneutical problem, but it was not one patristic exegetes were generally forced to deal with, precisely because they did not group texts in this way. They generally commented on one Gospel at a time, and while they often noted parallel passages, they did not do so in any systematic fashion. Certain Greek theologians, such as Origen and Chrysostom, did, however, confront the issue early on. Their basic solution was to make a distinction between the Pharisees who, because of their knowledge of scripture, had recognized Jesus as the Messiah, and the common run of first-century Jews, who had not. In this view, ordinary Jews had acted out of ignorance, but their leaders had maliciously crucified the Messiah. But the works of Origen and Chrysostom were not translated and widely circulated in western Europe until the late twelfth or early thirteenth century. As a result, western exegesis of these passages developed independently.[31] The Latin Fathers apparently made no attempt to reconcile them; commentators such as Augustine, Ambrose, and Gregory the Great did not distinguish between Jews who did and did not know Jesus was the Messiah. It was Bede who, in the early eighth century, introduced this interpretation. In his commentary on Luke 23.34, he claimed that Christ asked God to forgive only those who truly did not know what they did: the common people.[32] Bede's view was followed by a number of subsequent commentators, such as Rabanus Maurus and Paschasius Radbertus, though others, including Saint Anselm, did not adopt it.[33] It was the twelfth-century compilers of the *Glossa ordinaria* (a running commentary on the entire Bible that quickly became standard thoughout western Europe) who brought Bede's analysis into the mainstream. The *Glossa* repeated what Bede had said about Christ's prayer in Luke 23.34 and extended the same interpretation to I Corinthians 2.8. Notably, however, the *Glossa* made no effort to apply this interpretation to Acts 3.17, which specifically stated that the Jews *and* their leaders (*principes*) had acted out of ignorance. Also, the compilers of the *Glossa* subtly refined Bede's position by arguing that although the Jewish leaders had known Jesus was Christ, they had not understood that he was the incarnate Son of God. This directly contradicted Bede, who had claimed the priests and Pharisees knew Jesus was the *Filius Dei*.

Aquinas was in a position to draw on both the Greek and Latin traditions: he knew the *Glossa ordinaria* and Bede, of course, but he also read Origen and Chrysostom in translation and quoted their commentaries on Luke 23.34 in the *Catena Aurea*, his anthology of patristic exegesis. Faced with these various interpretations, Thomas typically opted for compromise.[34] Like the *Glossa*, his account relies on the distinctions between what the Jews and their leaders knew and between knowledge of Jesus as Messiah and as God. The *principes* knew Jesus was the savior; the masses only suspected this, and were eventually dissuaded by their leaders. On the question of whether or not the Jewish leaders knew Jesus was God, he tried to split the difference. He claims that while they were in a sense ignorant of Jesus' divine status, the *principes* were still guilty of deicide.

> It should be understood that their ignorance does not excuse the crime they committed, for their ignorance was in a sense affected. For they saw evident signs of his divinity, but out of hatred and envy they perverted both his miracles and his words, by means of which he proved himself to be the Son of God, in order that they might not believe in him.[35]

In Aquinas's view, the Jewish leaders had sufficient evidence to know that Jesus was divine, but they willfully refused to draw the conclusion. This increased rather than limited their culpability.

> Affected ignorance does not excuse guilt, but actually exacerbates it, for it shows that a man is so strongly attracted to sin that he wishes to remain ignorant so as not to avoid it. And thus the Jews sinned against Christ not only as a man—they also crucified God.[36]

Aquinas's argument here is strikingly tendentious. Certainly he knew that Jesus' claim to be the Son of God was no proof that he actually was divine, and he explicitly recognized that miracles can be deceptive: Demons, he wrote, as well as benevolent powers can perform acts that at least appear to be miraculous.[37] Aquinas was also well aware that the doctrine of the Incarnation was virtually incomprehensible to Jews, who were scandalized by Jesus' claim to be divine.[38] The matter is further complicated by the fact that, in his view, faith is a virtue infused by divine grace, and salvation is completely dependent on God's sovereign choice. But because Thomas was determined to uphold the Church's doctrine of Jewish guilt, he elided these complexities. Rather than bring the full logic of his ideas to bear on the problem, he settled for a synthesis of traditional views.

Even with the argument that the Jewish leaders acted *ex certa malitia* in place, however, Aquinas still had a ways to go to establish the perpetual guilt of all Jews.[39] After all, he admitted that the mass of Jews had not even known Jesus was the Messiah; in effect, they had acted out of good conscience.[40] Thus it was difficult to assert that they had incurred serious personal guilt. And the notion that medieval Jews were somehow responsible for Christ's death was even more problematic.

Aquinas's solution to these problems focused on the Resurrection. The Resurrection, he argued, made it clear who Jesus had been: By conquering death and ascending to heaven, Jesus proved he was truly Christ, the Son of God and the Savior of Israel. Yet the Jews refused to recognize this manifest reality. When the Jews assigned to guard the tomb reported that Jesus had risen, some believed them, but most did not. "Thus they sinned more, because they saw the miracle, yet did not believe he was able to rise again."[41] In the months and years that followed Jesus' ascension into heaven, many Jews, inspired by the preaching of the Apostles, accepted Christ.[42] Yet the majority remained hardhearted, and the Jewish leaders began to persecute the infant Church. Some even resorted to deceit. "After the death of Christ, many entered the Church in order to seize and ambush the holy ones."[43] By refusing to accept the evidence of Jesus' resurrection and by persecuting the Apostles, the Jewish people as a whole gave posthumous approval to the rejection of Christ. They also denied Christ by continuing to observe the Mosaic precepts. In performing the *caeremonialia*, the Jews asserted that the Messiah was still to come. For Aquinas, this ritual denial of Christ constituted mortal sin.[44]

Thomas goes on to argue that because they rejected Christ, the Jews were cast into spiritual exile. Cut off from the sole source of redemption, they incurred punishment not only for rejecting their Messiah, but also for original and positive sin. Prior to Christ, the observance of the Mosaic Law had been at least partially efficacious in remitting sin. Now, however, the Christian sacraments became the sole channel of grace, and performing the rituals of the *lex vetus* only added to the burden of Jewish guilt.

God, as always patient with his people, gave the Jews some forty years to repent of their wickedness. Then, in A.D. 70, he used the Emperor Titus and the might of Rome to crush the Jews and destroy their Temple, just as in days of old he had employed the Assyrians and Babylonians to punish Israel. When the Jews remained recalcitrant, Vespasian again subdued them in 135, then expelled them from Palestine. Already alienated from their God, the Jews now became physical exiles as they were gradually dispersed throughout the earth. And even though the generation that had witnessed the death of Jesus was long since gone, the Jews continued to be punished for his death, because their refusal to accept Christianity was a kind of approbation of the Crucifixion. Summing up this line of argument, Thomas wrote: "The blood of Christ binds the children of the Jews insofar as they are imitators of their parents' malice and thus approve of Christ's killing."[45]

Aquinas did not believe that all Jews rejected Jesus *ex certa malitia*. He knew they genuinely did not believe Jesus had been the Messiah, and he thought their unbelief was due, at least in part, to a spiritual blindness visited on them by God.[46] He also thought that Christians should pray for Jews; faith, after all, is a gift from God.[47] Nevertheless, like others who heard the gospel and did not accept it, he was convinced that the Jews' unbelief was gravely sinful.

> The ability to have faith is not a power of human nature. But it is natural that the mind not reject an interior impulse and the exterior preaching of truth. Thus, in a sense, unbelief is unnatural.[48]

Furthermore, the Jews added to their sin by actively denying Christ through their observance of the Mosaic Law. No longer the *verus Israel*, they were only a pathetic remnant, the carnal descendants of Abraham. Because their ignorance blinded them to the meaning of their own scriptures, the Jews were bound to perpetual servitude and degradation. From the perspective of sacred history, their continued existence was valuable only for the unwilling and inadvertent testimony their very misfortune gave to the truth of Christianity.

5. The Jews in Christian Society

> Si dicitur converso a Iudaeo infideli: Ubi est Deus tuus? Respondeat Iudaeus conversus ad fidem: Ubi est Deus meus apparet in poena vestra, scilicet Iudaeorum: quia estis dispersi.
>
> —*Super Psalmos* 41.2

Aquinas's teaching on the role of Jews in the Christian era rested on three theological pillars. The first of these was the doctrine whose development we traced in the previous chapter: the belief that the exile of the Jews was both a punishment for their role in the Crucifixion and a sign of the triumph of Christianity. Aquinas states the essence of his view in the epigraph above: "If an infidel Jew asks a convert: Where is your God? The convert should give this witness to the faith: The presence of my God is manifest in your punishment—that is, the punishment of the Jews—which is that you are dispersed."

The second pillar was Romans 11. Here Paul, seeking to forestall the development of Gentile triumphalism and contempt for Jews, had made it clear that the rejection of the Jews was temporary, that God still loved them, and that in time they would convert. What is more, he argued, this conversion would mean nothing less than "the resurrection of the dead" (Rm. 11.15). Thomas, reflecting on the experience of a thousand years of Christian missionary failure among Jews, sought to dampen the apostle's enthusiastic vision. Paul was exaggerating, he claimed; not every individual Jew would be saved. Nevertheless, he was certain that the Jews as a group would some day convert.

> It is possible to designate a terminus, because it seems that the blindness of the Jews will endure until all the pagans chosen for salvation have accepted the faith. And this is in accord with what Paul says below about the salvation of the Jews, namely, that after the conversion of the pagans, all Israel will be saved. "All" here does not mean each individual; rather, "all" Jews will be saved in a general sense.[1]

Following the Fathers and the *Glossa ordinaria*, Aquinas went on to explain that this mass conversion would be the catalyst for the *parousia*, the consummation of all human history in the Last Judgement.

The third theological pillar was the Augustinian theory that Christianity benefited from the continued presence of Jews. This theory claims that the dispersion of the Jews aids Christian missionary efforts, because their very existence lends credence to the argument that Jesus fulfilled Old Testament Messianic prophecies. True, the Jews do not accept this argument, but their presence guarantees the antiquity of the Hebrew scriptures on which it is based. Without the Jews' presence, pagans might regard Old Testament prophecies as ex post facto Christian fabrications.

> Because of their impenitence they have been scattered among all the nations. In this way Christ and the Church everywhere receive the testimony of Jewish books to the Christian faith, for the pagans might suspect that the prophecies of Christ—which preachers use to convert them—were forgeries, if the Jews did not testify to their authenticity.[2]

These theological doctrines directly influenced Aquinas's social teaching.[3] Thus he justifies the Jew's servile political and economic status on the grounds of the *culpa Iudaeorum*, the guilt the Jews incurred by crucifying Christ. The Jews are being punished by God, he claims, and their inferior status is part of that punishment. In drawing out the implications of Paul's hopeful vision of the ultimate conversion of the Jews, Aquinas manages to turn a positive into a negative. God, he claims, has ordained that the Jews remain blind to Christian truth until the end of time; hence missionary efforts among them are unlikely to bear fruit. At times, however, theology could work in favor of tolerance; for instance, Aquinas argues that Jewish worship should be permitted because of the inadvertent witness such worship gives to Christ.

But theology could serve only as a very broad guide to policy. Given both the generality and incommensurability of the dogmas pertaining to Jews, it was inevitable that other factors would determine the specific shape of law and social teaching in the High Middle Ages. The most important of these factors was fear of Jews.

Aquinas, like almost all Christians of his era, believed Jews were profoundly dangerous and that contact with them should be avoided whenever possible. In his writings on Jews, evidence of this fear manifests itself everywhere: Christians, he wrote, should not marry Jews, should not eat or socialize with them or conduct any business with them beyond what is absolutely necessary; ordinary Christians should never discuss religion with Jews, and even theologians should argue with Jews only under official auspices and in very controlled circumstances; Jews should not be allowed to hold Christian slaves or employ Christian servants, nor should they be permitted to hold any public office that would place them in a position of authority over Christians.

This horror of Jews was characteristic of the age. In its most dramatic and tragic manifestations, fear of Jews produced bizarre fantasies: some Christians believed that Jews desecrated the Eucharist, or that they killed Christian children and consumed their blood at their Passover feasts. Like the popes, Aquinas placed no credence in such crude myths. But these delusions—and the violence that stemmed from them—were rooted in a profoundly irrational fear of Jews which the official Church had done much to inculcate. In developing a body of social teaching that stigmatized Jews as dangerous pariahs, Aquinas did nothing more than articulate a systematized, apologetic version of the Church's position.

When popes, theologians, and secular rulers attempted to explain their fear of Jews, they pointed to the danger of apostasy, the possibility that Christians would convert to Judaism. Though some modern historians have dismissed this apprehension as illusory, it had some basis in fact. It is certain that many Jews who converted to Christianity later "relapsed" to their ancestral faith; the Fourth Lateran Council specifically addressed this issue, demanding that such converts be compelled to remain Christians.[4] But popes also mentioned people who had been born and reared as Christians and later converted to Judaism.

> With troubled heart we have heard, and now relate, that not only have some who were brought from Jewish blindness to the light of the Christian faith been known to perfidiously revert, but it is also true that a number of lifelong Christians have denied the truth of the Catholic faith and condemned themselves by adopting the Jewish rite. Such actions should be punished with particular severity because they give our enemies occasion to blaspheme the most sacred name of Christ.[5]

As Edward Synan has noted, it is unlikely that such references to Christian apostasy are completely unfounded.[6] Gregory X's letter also indicates a deeper source of the Church's chagrin: The vision of Jews mocking Christians and blaspheming Christ.

But a few instances of apostasy, however scandalous, do not explain the intense fear medieval Christians had of Jews. Nor do instances of judaizing, which was not a major problem, though there were occasional reports of Christians consulting rabbis. Syncretism and conversion to Judaism were, if anything, less frequent in the thirteenth century than they had been previously, and certainly there was nothing as spectacular as the ninth-century conversion of the deacon Bodo. Aquinas, commenting on Matthew 23.15, stresses the gravity of the sin committed by Christians who convert to Judaism, but also states that such cases were extremely rare ("paucissimi conversi sunt").[7] Yet in the thirteenth century a plethora of canons were promulgated which regulated all manner of Christian-Jewish relations and extended the Church's authority into entirely new areas, such as censorship of Jewish books and taking sides in doctrinal disputes among Jews. In an era when Jews represented less of an objective threat to Christianity than they ever had, Christians seemed more worried about them than ever.

One reason for this new activism was that, for the first time, the popes had the power, money, and bureaucratic apparatus they needed to regulate European Jews effectively. Before Innocent III (1198–1216), popes could only promulgate canons on the treatment of Jews and hope diocesan bishops and secular rulers would enforce them. But in the thirteenth century, popes did not always have to plead; sometimes they could coerce. To be sure, their reach often exceeded their grasp. An especially determined ruler could still protect "his" Jews from the pope. This was demonstrated by the defiant refusal of King James I of Aragon to punish Rabbi Moses ben Nachman for writing the *Vikuah*, a pro-Jewish account of his role in the Barcelona Disputation of 1263. But most rulers fell into line, partly out of respect for the papacy's new power and prestige, but also because an anti-Jewish policy had other benefits: pressuring Jews gave monarchs an aura of piety and helped curry favor with the Christian masses. In any case, after 1240 or so, the Holy See possessed a coercive bureaucracy of its own which it could bring to bear if the secular arm proved recalcitrant: the Roman Inquisition.

More efficient enforcement helps explain why canon law weighed ever more heavily on the Jews of thirteenth-century Europe. But the motives that lay behind the promulgation and enforcement of these laws must be explored more deeply. If instances of apostasy and judaizing do not sufficiently explain the fear and loathing of Jews expressed by ecclesiastical officials, political rulers, and ordinary Christians, what does?

Part of the answer lies in the growing resentment toward the Jews as "usurers," a resentment which, as was noted in Chapter 2, was rooted in the ambivalent attitude of Christians toward money and the new market economy.[8] Even more important, Jews were the most visible and notorious religious dissenters in an age that had little tolerance for such dissent. In the thirteenth century, powerful forces were working to make western Europe a united, ideologically uniform society. The papal monarchy, the Albigensian Crusades, the Inquisition, the explosive growth of the mendicant orders, and the efforts of intellectuals to achieve system and synthesis are all evidence of this basic impulse.[9] In this context, the continued resistance of Jews to the Christian gospel was an intolerable scandal. In the past, most Christians had shrugged their shoulders and attributed the Jews' recalcitrance to a mysterious spiritual blindness inflicted on them by God. Yet the refusal of Jews to convert constituted an implicit attack on Christianity, and in the thirteenth century many ecclesiastical officials, secular rulers, and even ordinary Christians were in no mood to countenance such an affront. Moreover, an emerging group of Christian Hebraists and the translation of works from Hebrew into Latin led to the growing realization that Jews were capable of producing harsh, explicit critiques of the Christian faith. The writings of Maimonides, for instance, not only offered an impressive rationalist interpretation of the Mosaic Law which made no reference to Christ, they also bristled with contemptuous references to Christianity. Many Talmudic passages also sounded blasphemous to Christian ears. And Jewish disputants like Moses ben Nachman had an annoying penchant for subverting orchestrated demonstrations of the truth of Christianity and publicly questioning the plausibility of the Church's teaching.

Such attacks rankled, because Jews hit Christianity where it was weakest. Many of their attacks focused on the person of Jesus. The putative savior, they pointed out, was sorely lacking in certain messianic attributes. The heir of David was supposed to restore Israel, yet just forty years after Jesus' death the Temple was destroyed by the Romans and the Jews were sent into exile. Christians, of course, responded to this line of criticism by interpreting these prophecies allegorically and arguing that Jesus has founded a spiritual kingdom. Other texts, however, could not be so easily sidestepped. For instance, Isaiah had prophesied that the coming of the Messiah would inaugurate an era of world peace (Is. 2.4). Clearly this had not occurred; in fact, as Rabbi Moses ben Nachman, or Nachmanides, mockingly pointed out to James I of Aragon at the Barcelona Disputation, Christians themselves did much to perpetuate the cycle of violence.

> From the days of Jesus until now, the whole world has been full of violence and plundering, and the Christians are greater spillers of blood than all the rest of the peoples. . . . And how hard it would be for you, my lord King, and for your knights, if they were not to learn war any more! [10]

Christians were sorely pressed to respond to this attack. The *Glossa Ordinaria* on Isaiah claimed that wars were less frequent since the coming of Christ. Aquinas, no doubt realizing how lame this assertion was, pushed the epoch of messianic peace back into the indefinite future, saying it would occur only at the time of the second coming.[11]

Jewish exegetes also criticized Christian prefigurative interpretations of the Hebrew scriptures.[12] To them, it was clear that Christians read the Bible backwards and arrogantly imputed meanings to the Hebrew text that no objective exegete would ever dream of. Christians responded to this charge in a variety of ways. Most blithely repeated patristic symbolic interpretations and rejected Jewish criticisms as just another manifestation of Jewish stupidity and blindness. By contrast, Andrew of St. Victor wrote a series of Old Testament commentaries which avoided Christological exegesis altogether, even when dealing with the "suffering servant" passages of Isaiah 52–53. Not surprisingly, he was subsequently attacked as a "judaizer."[13] William of Auvergne also avoided attributing Christological meanings to the Mosaic Law in his *De Legibus*. He was spared the criticisms Andrew had suffered, however, no doubt because he possessed impeccable anti-Jewish credentials. Aquinas adopted a middle position. He defended a prefigurative reading of the Law and Prophets, but at the same time he stressed that religious doctrine must be derived solely from the literal meaning of the Bible. Symbolic interpretation is edifying, he declared, but it cannot serve as the basis of dogma.[14]

Jews also criticized Christianity on philosophical grounds, claiming that doctrines such as the Trinity and the Virgin Birth were contrary to reason.[15] Such arguments were largely pro forma. From the time of Philo of Alexandria, Jewish thinkers had distinguished among a variety of divine attributes, and it took a subtle mind indeed to see why it was legitimate to posit a plurality of divine attributes yet blasphemous to speak of several divine persons within the unity of the Godhead.[16] A few Jews, such as Joseph Kaspi, even argued that Trinitarianism was compatible with traditional Judaism.[17] Similarly, since Jews recognized God's ability to perform miracles, it was hard for them to deny in principle the possibility of the Virgin Birth.

The true crux of the matter was the doctrine of the Incarnation. It might be possible to argue over the possibility of divine persons, but Jews knew God could not become a human being. For them, the claim that God had been born of a woman and had suffered and died was not merely false, it was repugnant and blasphemous. Of course, Jews were not the only ones who rejected the Incarnation. Pagan philosophers in the early centuries of the Christian movement had relentlessly attacked it, and it was a major stumbling block for missionaries trying to convert the Moslems. Even for Christians the doctrine was problematic. A long series of councils had been required to hammer out the orthodox doctrine. The Church declared that God had not become a human being as such, but that the divine nature had been joined to a human nature in a personal or "hypostatic" union. Christ was one person, but he possessed both a divine and a human nature. Still, the matter did not rest here. Dissenting Nestorian and Monophysite groups flourished for centuries in the Middle East, and Arianism was long a force in the West. Nor were the Middle Ages free of Christological controversy. There were active dissident movements in the twelfth and thirteenth centuries which denied that Jesus was divine. Even the orthodox had their uneasy moments; in 1140 Peter the Venerable wrote a treatise to ease the doubts of a group of monks who had noticed that Jesus never explicitly claimed to be God.

Jews also assailed the doctrine of the real presence of Christ in the Eucharist, which was formally defined and promulgated as dogma at the Fourth Lateran Council in 1215. They pointed out the obvious metaphysical problem of Christ's body being in two places at once, and wondered, tongue in cheek, why his flesh had not yet been completely consumed.[18] Such criticisms were nettlesome, because they echoed and reinforced Christians' own doubts. The 1215 definition had brought closure to more than three centuries of occasionally bitter debate, but at the same time it forced the faithful, at the peril of their immortal souls, to believe they literally consumed the flesh and blood of Jesus when they received communion. Many found it difficult to accept a dogma so at odds with common sense; witness John of Joinville's story about the theologian who came to William of Auvergne in tears, confessing his inability to believe in the real presence.

Aside from their criticisms of Catholic doctrine, the very existence of Jews was a scandal to Christians, for their refusal to convert reminded them that the truth of the Catholic faith was not as self-evident as they liked to think. And as Christians became increasingly aware of Judaism as an active spiritual and intellectual force, capable not only of defending itself but of attacking Christianity in ways disturbingly similar to the critiques of heretical groups, Jews appeared even more menacing. It is not surprising that Inquisitors were inclined to see Jewish influences behind Christian heretical movements, or that, in the late thirteenth century, some would begin to argue that Jews simply were heretics and should be treated as such.

Thomas Aquinas did not take this step. His discussion of Jews is notably free of any taint of hysteria. Just as there is no sign that he believed charges that Jews crucified Christian children, consumed the blood of Christians at Passover, or desecrated the Eucharist, so too did he never accused Jews of fomenting heresy, and he made it very clear that Jews were not to be treated as heretics. Nevertheless, Aquinas was firmly convinced that Jews were dangerous and that a Christian society was obligated to take elaborate precautions to guard against them.

The bulk of Aquinas's social teaching on Jews is contained in six articles of the *secunda secundae* of his *Summa Theologiae* (hereinafter *ST2–2*), 10.7–12.[19] The context of this discussion is important. Aquinas wrote his *Summa* in three parts. In Part One he dealt with God and creatures, in Part Two with "virtues, vices, and other things pertaining to morality,"[20] and in Part Three with Christ, the Church, and eschatology. Part Two is further subdivided into two parts, the *prima secundae* and the *secunda secundae*. The *prima secundae* is a kind of metaphysics of morals; in it Aquinas discusses in general terms the purpose of human life as well as the nature of volition, virtue, vice, law, and grace. The *secunda secundae* contains Thomas's analysis of particular virtues and vices.[21] In other words, the *prima secundae* serves as a theoretical preface to the more specific analyses of the *secunda secundae*.

Though intricate in execution, the plan of the *secunda secundae* is simple. It contains two basic parts: general virtues and vices (qq. 1–170), and those pertaining only to individuals in specific occupations, especially priests and members of religious orders (qq. 171–89). The first part is divided into seven sections, corresponding to the three theological virtues (faith [qq. 1–16], hope [qq. 17–22], and charity [qq. 23–46]) and the four cardinal virtues (prudence [qq. 47–56], justice [qq. 57–122], fortitude [qq. 123–40], and temperance [qq. 141–70]). Within each section, Aquinas analyzes the subordinate virtues related to these primary virtues as well as the vices contrary to them.

The articles that contain the bulk of Thomas's social teaching on Jews (*ST2–2* 10.7–12) are part of the section concerned with faith and the vices opposed to it. Question 10 is entitled "On Unbelief in General" (*De Infidelitate in Communi*), and it contains twelve articles.[22]

1. Is unbelief a sin?
2. Is the intellect the locus of unbelief?
3. Is unbelief the gravest sin?
4. Is every act performed by unbelievers sinful?
5. Are there several species of unbelief?
6. Is the unbelief of pagans or gentiles most gravely sinful?
7. Should Christians debate religion with unbelievers in public?
8. Should unbelievers be forced to accept Christianity?
9. Should Christians associate with unbelievers?
10. May unbelievers exercise *praelatio* or *dominium* over Christians?
11. Should unbelievers be allowed to worship?
12. Should the children of Jews or other unbelievers be baptized against their parents' wishes?

The title of the question as a whole, "On Unbelief in General," is significant. It indicates that, for Aquinas, the Jews' determining trait is their refusal to believe in Christ. By definition they are sinners; he discusses the treatment of Jews in the context of defining the nature and consequences of the sin of unbelief. Also, Jews are just one type of unbeliever. There is no question in the *Summa* entitled *De Iudaeis*. Unbelievers is the genus; Jews, heretics, and "gentiles" or "pagans" are the species.

Nevertheless, it quickly becomes clear that Jews are a special case. For Aquinas, there are two basic types of unbelievers: those who have never heard the Gospel, and those who have heard it and rejected it. Of course, those who have never had a chance to accept Christ cannot be blamed for their unbelief; people cannot believe in someone they have never heard of. All the same, these unbelievers will be damned, though not specifically for their lack of faith.

> For those who have heard nothing of the faith, unbelief is more a punishment than a sin, since it is a consequence of original sin. Hence while they will be damned for their other sins, which cannot be remitted without faith in Christ, such persons will not be condemned for the sin of unbelief.[23]

Jews, however, have heard the Gospel. Hence their failure to believe is sinful. What is more, their knowledge of the Law exacerbates their sin. Unlike pagans, it should be easy for them to recognize Jesus as the Messiah who was promised of old. Hence Jewish unbelief is more blameworthy than that of pagans who reject the Gospel: "Because they received it symbolically in the Old Law . . . their unbelief is more gravely sinful than the unbelief of pagans who have never received the Gospel in any sense."[24]

If personal guilt had been the only variable determining how Thomas thought unbelievers should be treated, Jews would have fared badly at his hands. Their knowledge of scripture made their rejection of the Gospel especially culpable, and Aquinas also believed the Jews were condemned to perpetual slavery because their ancestors had crucified Jesus. But, as it turned out, neither the culpability of Jewish unbelief nor the concept of the *servitus Iudaeorum* had much impact on Aquinas's social teaching. There were two reasons for this. First, he thought that protecting the faith, rather than carrying out divine retribution, should be the primary goal of Christian social policy. Second, he believed that natural justice placed definite limits on how Jews could be treated.

For Aquinas, the distinction between heretics and other unbelievers was absolute. Heretics had embraced the fullness of truth, then repudiated it. In doing so they broke their solemn vow to be faithful to Christ. This could not be allowed. Mother Church continued to love her wayward children, but she could not overlook the grave danger the heterodox posed both to the eternal salvation of ordinary believers and to the peace of Christian society. It was her duty to force heretics to accept the true faith; if they were recalcitrant, they must be turned over to the political authorities for execution.[25]

Jews and pagans were an entirely different case. Because they were in no way Christians, these unbelievers should "in no way be compelled to accept the faith."[26] Here Aquinas was quite self-consciously relying on canon law; elsewhere in the same article he quotes a passage from Gratian's *Decretum* which forbids forcing Jews to convert.[27] His rationale was also traditional. Faith is by its very nature voluntary; hence a coerced faith is no faith at all.

It should be noted that Aquinas was relying on a tenuous distinction in separating Jews from heretics. Given his ideas about the prefigurative function of the Law, his extraordinary claim that some Jews in the era before the Incarnation had possessed an explicit faith in Christ, and his belief that even ordinary Jews had professed an implicit belief in him each time they obeyed one of the Law's ceremonial precepts, it would have been quite logical for Aquinas to have argued that Jews *had* accepted the Christian faith; after all, they had "received its symbol (*figura*) in the Old Law."[28] Clearly a great deal rides on this distinction between accepting a symbol of the faith and acknowledging its reality. But Aquinas's notion of what Old Testament Jews believed does not precisely fit the symbol/reality dichotomy. Abraham, Joseph, Moses, David, and other wise and pious Jews explicitly believed in Christ; the Pharisees and priests knew Jesus was the Messiah. One of the consequences of Aquinas's efforts to stress the continuity between the Old and New Testaments should have been a blurring of the distinction between Jews and heretics.

Yet Thomas does not make this move. This fact limns the fundamental cleavage between his theological views and his social teaching. Aquinas's social teaching on Jews is not a matter of drawing practical conclusions from theological premises; indeed, Aquinas drew back from a number of conclusions that logically followed both from his theology and from his belief that Jews were potentially dangerous. One reason for this is that his social teaching on Jews is primarily an apologia for the contemporary practice of the institutional Church. The conclusions are given; the problem is to find reasons to support them. Hence Aquinas uses bits and pieces of his theological teaching in an ad hoc manner to defend the Church's treatment of Jews. This helps account for the apparently random and disjointed character of Aquinas's views which Hans Liebeschutz pointed out.[29]

Another reason Aquinas's social teaching on Jews is largely detached from his theological ideas is that scripture and the Christian theological tradition were not the only influences on Aquinas's ethical thinking. Aristotle was also important, as was the Roman law tradition. In his social teaching on the Jews, Aquinas was at times clearly moving toward a more tolerant paradigm, a paradigm in which basic rights and principles of natural justice would outweigh theological considerations. Thomas himself, of course, believed that "grace perfects nature"—that philosophy and theology complement each other. But in Aquinas's thought this principle is often honored more in the breech than the observance. As some of his contemporaries pointed out, the Greek and Christian world-views did not dovetail as neatly as Aquinas pretended they did, and modern scholars have shown that the Thomist system is rife with latent tensions between Christian theology and Aristotelian rationalism. At times Aquinas's ideas on how Jews should be treated are more firmly rooted in philosophical ethics than in theological principles.

This rationalism may have influenced Aquinas's argument that Jews and other unbelievers should "in no way" be compelled to accept Christianity. In the twelfth and thirteenth centuries there was considerable debate over what exactly constituted compulsion. The question arose mostly in the context of anti-Jewish violence: Were Jews who had converted to save their lives required to live as Christians? Popes and canon lawyers were inclined to say yes. Responding in 1201 to a series of queries from the

Bishop of Arles, Innocent III stretched the notion of "voluntary conversion" about as far as it could go.

> Those who unwillingly and reluctantly were baptized do come under ecclesiastical jurisdiction because of the sacrament and hence may reasonably be compelled to observe the rules of the Christian faith. It is true that it is contrary to the Christian religion that anyone who is unwilling and completely opposed should be forced to receive and observe Christianity. This is why it is not absurd to distinguish between different degrees of unwillingness and coercion. Thus one brought to baptism by violence—fearful, begging for mercy, and hoping to avoid loss—does truly receive the sacrament . . . [and] is in fact a Christian, since he expressed a certain conditional willingness to be baptized, although he did not will it in an absolute sense. Such a person should be forced to observe Christianity . . . lest the name of the Lord be blasphemed and the faith be considered vile and held in contempt. On the other hand, he who in no way consented, but wholly objected, receives neither the sacrament itself nor the character it imparts, because explicit objection is different from giving even minimal consent.[30]

Aquinas was no stranger to such fine distinctions. In the *Summa Theologiae* he argued that, no matter how narrowly circumscribed the conditions, an action is not, strictly speaking, involuntary as long as there are at least two options from which to choose.[31] From this he could have concluded that Jews and other unbelievers who chose baptism over death acted voluntarily. But Aquinas does not distinguish between licit and illicit forms of coercion when it comes to forced conversion; rather, "in nullo modo" are unbelievers to be compelled. The phrase may have been a protest, albeit a very subtle one, against the kind of self-serving casuistry Innocent employed. On the other hand, he never dealt directly with the question of how forced converts should be treated, and he certainly shared Innocent's concern about the possibility of Christ being blasphemed and the faith brought into contempt. As usual, if Thomas had doubts about the Church's policy, he kept them to himself.

Rationalism played a much more explicit role when Aquinas turned to the question of whether or not the children of Jews and other unbelievers should be baptized against their parents' will. Several bits of evidence suggest that this was very much a live question in the early 1270s. One is that Thomas poses and deals with five objections in dealing with this issue. (The article is entitled "Should the children of Jews or other unbelievers be baptized against their parents' wishes?") In general, whenever a *Summa* article contains more than three objections it is a sign that the question at hand is either controversial or especially knotty. Second, Aquinas refers to the claim that Jewish children should be baptized as a "new assertion" because it was contrary to the traditional practice of the Church. Presumably, an assertion implies an asserter. Also, precisely the same issue is addressed later, at *Summa Theologiae Tertia Pars* 68.10, in the context of a general discussion of baptism, while a doublet of the earlier article appears among Aquinas's quodlibetal questions. Quodlibetal questions usually dealt with topical or controversial issues.[32] Finally, we know that twenty years after Aquinas's death Duns Scotus openly advocated forced baptism of Jewish children. It seems reasonable to presume Scotus had precursors.[33]

Aquinas's approach to this question is typically conservative. It would be perilous, he argues, to introduce such a practice when for centuries it had not been the Church's custom to baptize Jewish children against their parents' wishes. Look at Pope Sylvester I and Bishop Ambrose, he suggests: Given their close friendship with the Roman emperor, these wise and holy men certainly would have called for legislation mandating this practice, if it were in accord with reason.

Aquinas goes on to provide two *rationes* for the Church's traditional position. First, he argues that such a practice would endanger the faith. If the children of Jews were baptized, in later years they might well be induced by their parents to embrace Judaism, "which would tend to undermine the faith."

His second argument is more elaborate. Baptizing Jewish children, Thomas claims, would be contrary to natural justice (*iustitia naturalis*).

> A child naturally belongs to its father. At first, when the child is not physically distinct from its parents, it is contained in its mother's womb. After birth, however, and before it has the ability to make free choices, it continues to be in its parents' care; the child still lives in a kind of "womb," albeit a spiritual one. . . . Hence, under natural law, the child, before it reaches the age of reason, remains under its father's care. Therefore it would violate natural justice to take such a child from its parents, or to mold the child spiritually in a way contrary to the parents' wishes.[34]

The child, Thomas argues, belongs to its parents in the strongest possible sense. He is their flesh and blood, and it is their responsibility—and their right—to provide him with spiritual guidance. For Aquinas, as for Aristotle, justice means giving each his due. Allowing parents to raise their children as they see fit is simply giving them their due; to take their children from them or to interfere in their ability to provide spiritual instruction would be unjust. This line of thought implicitly forestalls a possible objection to the previous argument that Jewish children should not be baptized because they might later revert to Judaism. An obvious solution to this problem would be to take the children from their parents and raise them with a Christian family, or perhaps in a monastery. Clearly, however, this would doubly violate natural justice, according to Aquinas's definition.

It is important to note that this argument against baptizing Jewish children is essentially nontheological. True, Aquinas invokes the force of ecclesiastical tradition, but this tradition is then defended on purely rational grounds: such baptisms would be imprudent and would violate *natural* justice. There were two reasons Aquinas chose to argue from natural law premises. The first was his belief that no considerations, however weighty, could make an action licit if it were contrary to natural law. The second was that he had no choice. There was absolutely nothing in Aquinas's theology of Judaism that could have served as a premise in an argument against baptizing Jewish children.

On the contrary, there were a number of theological arguments that could be marshalled in *favor* of forcible baptisms of Jewish children. Five such arguments serve as objections to Aquinas's position in *secunda secundae* 10.12. In each case, Aquinas replies to a theological argument with a reply based on natural justice. Of these objections, numbers 2–4 are the most important.[35]

The second objection is based on an analogy: Since it is wrong not to come to the aid of someone in danger of dying, it is even worse not to aid the children of Jews—who are in danger of eternal damnation—by baptizing them. Aquinas meets this analogy with another one. Just as one should not violate civil law in order to save someone justly condemned to death ("a suo iudice condemnetur ad mortem temporalem"), nor should one violate natural law, which commits children to their parents' care, in order to save them from eternal death. This reply is remarkable in two respects. First, it reveals the astonishing depth of his commitment to natural law. Aquinas in effect argues that it is better to allow a child to suffer eternal torment than to violate natural justice. Second, the argument itself is notably weak, because the analogy does not hold. Rescuing a condemned criminal violates civil law by directly contravening a duly rendered punishment. Baptizing a child against its parents' wishes is different; it is in danger of eternal death not because of any *personal* guilt, but because it has inherited original sin and can only be redeemed by Christ's grace, which flows through the sacrament of baptism. In other words, rescuing a condemned criminal from execution prevents him from receiving his due according to civil justice, whereas baptizing the child of Jewish parents does not undermine justice vis-à-vis the child. True, the child "deserves" damnation because of original sin, but so do all children—and certainly baptism per se is not contrary to justice. Here the just order being violated is not between the person in peril and the punishment due him, as in the case of the condemned criminal, but between the person in peril (the child) and his parents. A closer analogy would seem to obtain between a child and its Jewish parents and a child whose parents neglected or abused it until it was in danger of physical death. Yet surely in the latter case a child should be removed from his parents' care; why not in the former?

Aquinas's reply to the fifth objection provides a clue to the answer. Again, the objection stems from an analogy: just as it is a sin not to preach the Gospel which could bring salvation to others, so too it is wrong to refrain from saving Jewish children through baptism. Aquinas replies that a person is guilty of not preaching if and only if it is his duty, his *officium*, to preach. Similarly, it is parents who are responsible for having their children baptized. If they fail to do this, the guilt is theirs. Thomas's position thus rests on a very rigid conception of the parental role: Parents alone are accountable for their children's welfare. The larger society is entirely absolved of responsibility.

The same conception governs his reply to the third objection. This objection is based on the theological doctrine of the *servitus Iudaeorum*:[36] Jews are slaves of the prince, therefore no injustice is done if the secular ruler orders Jewish children to be baptized against their parents' will. Aquinas rebuts this in a single sentence: "The Jews are slaves of the prince under civil servitude, which does not exclude the order of natural or divine law." Thus even slave owners cannot control—nor are they responsible for—the spiritual development of the children they own.

What has gone before is remarkable enough, but it is only in his reply to the fourth objection that the full scope of Aquinas's notion of parental rights and responsibilities becomes completely evident. There is a certain progression to the queries the objections pose: Should people in general intervene to secure the baptism of the children of Jews? Should the secular rulers, who own them and are generally responsible for the common good? In each case the answer was no. Now the ultimate question is posed.

> Everyone belongs more to God, from whom he received his soul, than to his parents, from whom he received his body. Hence it would not be unjust to

> take the children of Jews from their physical parents in order to consecrate them to God.[37]

After considering the responsibility of society and the rights of princes, Thomas invokes God's *dominium*. Surely nothing could be as significant as the child's relationship with God? Perhaps, Aquinas replies, but the natural order still cannot be violated.

> Man is related to God by his reason, through which he knows God. Thus a child, prior to the age of reason, is naturally related to God through the reason of his parents, to whose care he is naturally subject, and it is according to their wishes that he is to be instructed on religious matters.[38]

Aquinas stands his ground: The parent-child bond is inviolable, even if the consequences include allowing the child to suffer eternal alienation from God. From a twentieth-century perspective, of course, Aquinas's steadfastness seems admirable, for the alternative is totalitarian. But in the context of the medieval world-view, and even of his own thought, his position is difficult to explain. Aquinas was in all sincerity advocating that children be allowed to burn in hell rather than permit society to violate the rights of parents. If we moderns took hell as seriously as we take child abuse, his attitude would appear monstrous. No doubt his position reflects his deep commitment to natural law and his absolutist insistence that no consequence, however heinous, can justify a morally wrong act. But medieval natural law theory was not handed down at Sinai along with the Ten Commandments; thinkers disagreed over its nature and its requirements. Duns Scotus also believed in natural law, and he simply invoked hierarchy to conclude that Jewish children should be baptized: God's *dominium* supersedes all others, including that of parents.[39] There was nothing in Aquinas's view of natural law to prevent him from taking a similar view. At bottom, his position appears arbitrary; in Thomistic terms it is more like a *determinatio*, the act of making the best possible prudential judgment given the circumstances, than a straightforward deduction from first principles. No doubt he was drawn to this position by his determination to defend the traditional practices of the Church. It may also be that, at an intuitive level, Aquinas simply felt it was wrong to take children from their parents.

On the issue of Jewish worship, as on forced conversion and baptism of Jewish children, Aquinas adopted a relatively tolerant position. But whereas he had opposed forcing any non-Christian to convert or have his children baptized—not just Jews—he argued that Jews alone should have freedom of worship in a Christian society. Pagan rites, he believed, should not be tolerated except in extraordinary circumstances. His argument for this position is basically Augustinian. Just as God permits evil in the universe, either to attain a greater good or to avoid more serious evil, so the Church and temporal rulers should allow Jews to worship according to the Law, despite the fact that their rituals are sinful.

> When the Jews observe their rituals, which at one time prefigured the truths of our faith, this good result follows: we receive a testimony to the truth of our faith from our enemies, and in a sense what we believe is symbolically manifested to us. Hence their rituals should be tolerated.[40]

Like his opposition to forced conversion and baptism of Jewish infants, Aquinas's position on freedom of worship for European Jews is essentially conservative: he argues in support of a traditional privilege that Jews possessed under canon law. But this time the nature of his arguement is strikingly different. Here Thomas does not appeal to natural law, nor does he base his case for toleration on the inviolability of the will or the duty to follow the dictates of conscience. Aquinas believed in these principles, but he did not appeal to them in defending the Jews' freedom of worship. The reason is clear: it would have been impossible for him to develop a natural law argument for freedom of worship that would apply only to Jews. On the contrary, an argument based on natural law principles would have entailed letting pagans, and perhaps heretics, worship God as they saw fit. To avoid such a conclusion Aquinas fell back on a pragmatic, theological argument: permitting Jews to observe the Law helps promote the Christian faith.

This move highlights the ambiguity characteristic of Aquinas's intellectual position. His belief in the validity and power of natural reason, unaided by revelation, made it possible for him to turn to pagan thinkers such as Aristotle, Moslems such as Averroes and Avicenna, and Jews such as Maimonides, in search of philosophical wisdom. These men did not possess the light of Christian truth, but Thomas was convinced that Christians could learn much from them within certain spheres. In approaching non-Christian writings, Aquinas consistently avoided those issues where the texts were incompatible with Christian faith. Instead he confined his attention to areas of common ground, where he could learn from a pagan,

Moslem, or Jew without compromising his Christian faith. In principle, this method could have been applied to social relations as well. But not in 1270. The vision of an ideologically uniform Christian society was too compelling, and Church and state were too closely intertwined. At times the inner logic of Aquinas's thought pointed in the direction of greater tolerance and a more naturalistic paradigm. When possible—as on the issues of forced conversion and baptism—he followed this bent and looked to natural law for principles governing Jewish-Christian relations. But when the implications of natural law directly conflicted with the existing social order, Aquinas abandoned philosophy and turned to theological principles that would bolster the status quo.

Yet even here there were tensions, for Aquinas's theology of Judaism and his social teaching were not perfectly matched. Specifically, it is hard to see how Thomas's argument for tolerating Jewish worship makes much sense, even on theological grounds.

Aquinas stated explicitly in *Summa Theologiae Secunda Secundae* 10.11 that he thought the inadvertent testimony Jewish worship gave to Christian truth was analogically related to the prefigurative function of the *caeremonialia*: actions that had once foreshadowed future events now symbolize present realities, that is, Christ and his redemptive work. For symbols to be meaningful, however, someone must understand them. Aquinas solves this problem adroitly. Once the *sapientes* among the Jews understood the prophetic significance of the Mosaic rituals, but now it is Christians—the new *sapientes*—who understand their true meaning. But symbols must also be perceived if they are to signify, and Thomas does not make it clear just how Christians were supposed to observe Jews performing the symbolic rituals of the Law. For one thing, he claimed that Jews performed only a limited set of rituals since the destruction of the Temple.[41] Animal sacrifice, which Christian exegetes saw as a "type" of Jesus' redemptive death, was a thing of the past, as was the Levitical priesthood. Of the *caeremonialia*, only circumcision, the dietary laws, and holy festivals such as Passover remained to "symbolize" Christian truth. But how could Christians perceive these practices? Canon law forbade them from attending a circumcision rite, observing Passover, or even sharing a meal with Jews, and certainly Thomas did not call for the repeal of such prohibitions. To be sure, Christians could study the Pentateuch (or rather those who read Latin could) in order to see the connections between Old Testament *caeremonialia* and Christianity. But they did not need actual Jews in their midst to do this.

Though the Church's segregationist policies largely undermined Aquinas's rationale for tolerating Jewish worship, other aspects of his apologia for the Church's social teaching were more compatible with his theological views. He was certain that, unless and until they repented and accepted Christ, the Jews were damned. As such, like all unbelievers, they are potentially threatening, for if a Christian falls under their influence he will lose his own salvation. And Jews are especially dangerous, because they do have something in common with Christians—the belief that the Hebrew scriptures were inspired by God. This makes religious discussion and disputation possible, since it gives Christians and Jews a common text, but it also makes it perilous. Aquinas knew it was not easy to understand how Christ fulfilled the messianic prophecies of the Old Testament. The text was often enigmatic; various levels of meaning had to be distinguished, and there were troublesome passages that had to be explained away. Most Christians were illiterate and hence could not begin to interpret scripture, and of those who could read, few were trained exegetes. For these and other reasons, ecclesiastical authorities were convinced that social contact between Christians and Jews was dangerous. Aquinas agreed, and he wholeheartedly supported the efforts of the institutional Church to limit such contacts.

Medieval canon law did not attempt to eliminate all interaction between Christians and Jews. The Church sought to protect the faith, not establish a system of apartheid. To some extent this policy was perfectly reasonable; given the fact that most bishops, priests, and theologians sincerely believed that only Christians could avoid eternal damnation, these officials would have been irresponsible if they had not worked to avoid apostacy. If the Church had designed its Jewish policy with the sole aim of preventing Christians from converting to Judaism, the strictures of that policy would not have been terribly onerous for Jews. But for medieval churchmen, defending the faith involved more than preventing apostasy; conciliar and papal decrees endlessly reiterated the need to avoid scandal and blasphemy as well. Anything that could bring the faith into disrepute or give the impression that Jews were better or more privileged than Christians was to be avoided. The goal was not only to deprive Jews of any opportunity to proselytize, but to insure that no contact between Christian and Jew should cause a Christian to feel ashamed or belittled. Thus, for example, canon law prohibited Christians from sharing a meal with Jews because this might lead them to adopt Jewish dietary laws, but it also proscribed purchasing certain foods from Jews, especially meat and wine. The latter prohibition was not designed to prevent judaizing; rather, it followed from the belief that Jews might try to sell Christians meat and wine that were of poor quality or perhaps ritually "unclean" according to Mosaic Law. For Christians, of course, no food was unclean, and presumably they were competent to judge the quality of the goods they purchased. Nevertheless, Pope Innocent III thought it was inappropriate for Christians to eat what Jews rejected, since he believed it implied a kind of inferiority. Writing in 1208 to the Count of Nevers, Innocent lambasted such practices.

> A scandal of some consequence to the Church of Christ is caused by the fact that, while they regard meat slaughtered by Christians as unclean and refuse to eat it, Jews obtain from princes the privilege of having Jewish slaughterers produce the meat according to their ritual, then take of this meat as much as they desire, leaving the rest for Christians. . . . No less detestable to Christians is another Jewish presumption: At the vintage season they trod the grapes wearing linen boots and after having extracted the wine they regard as purer, they leave the rest, as if it were befouled, for Christians. On occasion such wine has even been used at Mass.[42]

Aquinas did not deal with this type of social regulation in the *Summa Theologiae*; no doubt he realized that such issues would have led him into a quagmire of detail. Instead he restricted himself to three broad issues: The general problem of social contact between Christians and Jews, the issue of Jews holding positions of authority or dominance over Christians, and the Church's regulation of religious disputations. Nevertheless, he made it clear that he shared the belief that social policy should protect the honor of the faith as well as prevent Jewish proselytizing.

At *Summa Theologiae Secunda Secundae* 10.9, Aquinas distinguished two reasons for prohibiting social contact: either as a means of punishing someone, or in order to protect Christians. One common way of eliminating social interaction—excommunication—is a purely spiritual punishment, Thomas notes, and hence it would be inappropriate to use it against Jews and pagans, who have not accepted Christianity. Here he follows the ancient principle, based on I Corinthians 5.12, that the Church does not have spiritual dominion over outsiders ("de his qui foris sunt").[43] But Aquinas goes on to note that the Church does sometimes limit contact between Christians and Jews in order to protect the faith. The guiding principle is simple: Is such contact more likely to lead to Christian apostasy or to the conversion of Jews? If the conversion of Jews seems probable, social intercourse should be unlimited; if Christian apostasy is feared, contacts are to be kept to a minimum.

> It seems there should be distinctions according to the type of person involved, the business to be transacted, and the time. If someone is firm in the faith and there is more reason to hope for the conversion of the unbeliever than to fear apostasy, then there is no need to limit social contact between such Christians and either Jews or pagans, especially if there is good reason for it. On the other hand, if people are ignorant and their faith is tenuous to the point that social contact with unbelievers could undermine it, such contact should be prohibited. This prohibition should apply very strictly to frequent or intimate contacts and to any unnecessary communication.[44]

Aquinas restricts legitimate Jewish-Christian contact to two types: those that may lead to the conversion of Jews, and those stemming from the economic needs of Christians. This social calculus highlights the medieval Church's essentially manipulative attitude toward Jews. If Jews could be won for Christ, well and good; if there was something to be gained from them, contact was permissible. Otherwise they were to be shunned.

At *Summa Theologiae Secunda Secundae* 10.10, Aquinas goes on to argue that economic relations should also be carefully controlled. He believes it is acceptable for Christian laborers to work for Jewish employers as long as there is no danger of apostasy, but under no circumstances should Jews or pagans acquire ***dominium*** over Christians; that is, Jews should not be able to obtain Christian slaves or vassals.[45] Aquinas is explicit and realistic in his justification of this prohibition: subordinates are often inclined to adopt the views of their superiors. For a different reason, unbelievers should not be able to hold any office that would involve exercising authority of judgment over Christians. "Unbelievers will come to despise the faith if they know the faults of Christians." Aquinas relies on the principle that the honor of the Christian faith must be upheld, even when there is no danger of apostasy. Like many medieval churchmen, Thomas had a horror of Jews laughing at Christians.

Aquinas also believed that disputations—public religious debates—should be carefully circumscribed. By the middle of the thirteenth century, formal disputations were a recognized, if still marginal, part of Christian missionary strategy; Dominicans had disputed with Cathars in Languedoc in the 1220s, and Pablo Christiani's efforts to use the Talmud as a missionary tool relied on disputations with rabbis. As it turned out, disputations were usually ineffective in winning converts, but this was not yet clear in

1270, and the question of which types of disputation should be allowed was very much a live issue. It was generally agreed that the truth of Christianity should never be subject to debate. Rather, the non-Christian debator—whether heretic, Jew, Moslem, or pagan—must always be kept on the defensive. If this principle had always been followed in practice, it would have meant that disputations would have only been conducted in areas under Christian rule, and in cases where secular rulers were willing to force non-Christians to participate in the dispution. Only political power could have assured such control of the agenda of a disputation, and only coercion could have convinced non-Christians to engage in a debate under such unequal conditions. In fact, of course, many disputations were not so carefully controlled; for instance, Christian missionaries working in Provence in the early thirteenth century often had to debate with Cathars on more or less equal terms. But, since Jews were politically powerless, disputations with them were another matter. The Latin record of the Barcelona disputation illustrates the restraints placed on Jews who were forced to dispute publicly with Christians.

> [The disputation was held] not in order that the faith in the Lord Jesus Christ, which because of its certitude should not be put into dispute, should be drawn into the arena with the Jews as if it were a matter of doubt, but that the truth of that faith should become manifest in order to destroy the errors of the Jews.[46]

Aquinas's strictures closely follow the Barcelona model: "It is not proper to dispute about matters concerning faith as if they were in doubt, but only in order to make the truth manifest and to refute errors."[47] As an experienced academic debater, however, Thomas knew the course of a live debate could not be completely controlled; if unbelievers were to be allowed to defend themselves at all they would inevitably criticize Christianity. Hence he called for further restrictions. Not only should the faith not be treated as a matter of doubt, but the needs of the audience should be carefully considered. In areas where there were no unbelievers, disputations should not be conducted before ordinary Christians. No good can come of them, Thomas felt, and the spectacle of a religious debate could be damaging to the faith of the simple. His matter-of-fact observation was sensible, though it sounds ominous to modern ears: "The faith of the ignorant is firmer if they never hear anything that conflicts with what they believe."[48]

Aquinas does endorse disputations in front of general audiences in certain circumstances, but more as a means of apologetics than as a missionary tool. When Christians are subjected to missionary efforts or other attacks on their faith by unbelievers, he says, qualified disputants should be recruited to defend the faith. But Thomas does not discuss holding disputations before audiences of Jews or other unbelievers. It is impossible to know for certain what he thought of Pablo Christiani's missionary efforts, but his failure to mention this type of disputation is one of several bits of evidence that indicate he may not have approved of them. Others include the contemptuous tone of Aquinas's few references to the Talmud (the compilation of Jewish law which Christiani drew on for most of his arguments), and the fact that when, at Raymond de Peñafort's prompting, Thomas wrote the *Summa Contra Gentiles* to help missionary efforts in Spain, he adopted a philosophical approach and made no mention of using Jewish or Moslem literature. Most telling of all is an offhand comment in his *Commentary on Romans*. Explicating Paul's belief that, after the pagans have accepted Christianity, the Jews will be converted as well (Rm. 11.25–26), Aquinas expresses a decidedly pessimistic view of contemporary efforts to convert the Jews. When Paul quotes a text from Isaiah (59.20–21) which says that a redeemer will come from Zion "who will snatch away, and remove impiety from Jacob" ("qui eripiat, et avertat impietatem a Iacob"), Thomas interprets the passage as referring to two different times.

> It says "who will snatch away," because of the few who are converted now with difficulty and a certain amount of violence. . . . It says, however, "remove impiety from Jacob" to show the ease with which Jews will be converted at the end of time.[49]

This passage is tantalizing: Did Aquinas believe Christiani's methods were coercive? In any case, he clearly thought they had little chance of success.

To summarize, *Summa Theologiae Secunda Secundae* 10.7–12 is a general apologia for the Church's social policy, supplemented with special consideration of a few questions which were controversial or in which Aquinas was especially interested. His thoroughly conservative perspective is guided by the *Sicut* principle: Jews should be kept in their place, but their traditional privileges should also be preserved. In arguing for a continuation of those privileges—freedom from forced conversion, the right to raise their children as Jews, freedom of worship—Aquinas grounds his arguments in natural law reasoning whenever possible. By contrast, in supporting a variety of restrictions on Jews, he relies on theological premises and on the general principle that political rulers and ecclesiastical officials should do everything possible to protect the faith, a principle that makes it imperative Christians be protected from close contact with Jews. Though Aquinas's position is not entirely coherent on theological grounds, the basic picture is clear. Jews should be allowed to exist in peace, but, except in missionary situations, Christians' relations with Jews should be purely utilitarian and economic.

A brief comparison of Aquinas's social teaching on Jews with another contemporary analysis will help highlight both the traditional and the more innovative aspects of Thomas's thinking. A Franciscan *Summa Theologica*, composed in the late 1230s and early 1240s and attributed to Alexander of Hales, the first Franciscan professor on the theology faculty at the University of Paris, also contained a section dealing with the status of Jews in Christian society. This *Summa* reached final form some twenty-five years before Aquinas began his own magnum opus; he knew the work well, and it was among the theology textbooks he hoped his own *Summa* would supplant. Aquinas and his Franciscan counterpart were in general agreement on how Jews should be treated. Both believed Jews should continue to exist in Europe; both believed they should be allowed to practice their religion and that they should not be forcibly converted to Christianity. And both *Summae* stress insuring Jews remain subordinate to Christians and guarding against extensive social contacts. These conclusions were givens; they were the constants of Catholic social policy, which had been formulated in *Sicut Iudaeis* in 1122 and reinforced by dozens of later canons collected in Gratian's *Decretum* and Gregory IX's *Decretales*. The differences between Aquinas and his Franciscan counterpart were differences not of basic principles, but of how those principles were to be justified and then applied to specific social issues.

To some extent, these contrasts are simply a reflection of time and circumstance. For example, we find in the Franciscan work a query on the Talmud: Since the Talmud contains blasphemies against Christ and the Virgin Mary, how can Jews be tolerated?[50] Clearly this was a burning issue in the context of the Paris Talmud trial of 1240. Aquinas, by contrast, does not mention the Talmud at all in his discussion of Jews. His silence probably reflects the fact that, by the 1260s, the popes had (temporarily) lost interest in suppressing the Talmud, while the Christiani/Marti strategy of using the Talmud as a missionary tool may have made the work seem less threatening. In any case, for Aquinas, writing in Paris in 1272, the Talmud was not a particularly important issue in Jewish-Christian relations. On the other hand, new questions were being raised: Aquinas devotes articles to religious disputations and the possibility of baptizing Jewish children against their parents' wishes, issues that apparently did not occur to the Paris Franciscans of the early 1240s but that arose in the context of the more intensive missionary efforts among Jews conducted in the 1260s and 1270s.

There are methodological differences as well. The reasoning of the Franciscan *Summa* is basically canonistic. The nine questions grouped under the rubric *De Iudaeis et Paganis* are studded with canon law citations, many of them to the *Decretales*, which had just been issued in 1239. These citations give the questions the air of a legal commentary. This impression is reinforced by the general method of the Franciscan work, which is to cite and then attempt to reconcile the major relevent canons, as well as by the practical and specific nature of some of the issues addressed. For example, the Franciscan *Summa* discusses whether converts should be quickly received into the Church, and whether Jews can be compelled to pay tithes on income generated from property once owned by Christians.[51] (The answers: Baptism may be expedited or delayed at the discretion of the bishop; Jews may be required to pay tithes unless their income is derived from usury.) At times even the substantive reasoning smacks of lawyerly hair-splitting, as in the discussion of the difference between "absolutely" and "conditionally" forced conversions.[52]

Aquinas's approach, as we have seen, is quite different. His perspective is broadly theological and, at times, philosophical. He too cites authorities, but his authorities are of a different sort: the Bible and Aristotle. In the six articles he devotes to various aspects of Jewish-Christian relations, he refers to canon law on only five occasions. By contrast, the nine relevent *capitulae* of the Franciscan work contain forty-eight legal citations. In sum, whereas the questions of the Franciscan *Summa* are largely devoted to reconciling diverse canons and justifying them in terms of legal or biblical authorities, Aquinas was interested in defending the Church's policy by arguing from first principles. As a result, his discussion provides a much more comprehensive view of the place Jews occupied in the medieval Christian world-view, and, unwittingly, reveals more clearly the ambiguities that world-view contained.

Aside from the issue of Jews holding *dominium* over Christians, Aquinas had little to say in the *Summa Theologiae* specifically about the political and economic status of Jews in Christian Europe. Fortunately, his so-called *De Regimine Iudaeorum* helps fill this gap.

The traditional title of this brief document is doubly misleading. First, it implies a systematic treatise. In fact, however, the *De Regimine* is simply a letter containing Aquinas's replies to eight queries posed to him in 1271 by Marguerite, the daughter of King Louis IX of France, who was Countess of Flanders from 1244 to 1286 and a patroness of the Dominican Order. The title also indicates that "rule of Jews" is the primary topic. But only five of the eight questions posed have anything to do with Jews, and of the 211 lines the work contains in the Marietti edition, only 94 concern Jews.[53] What is more, three of those five questions are concerned with a single theme: usury. The relevant issue in these questions, as Thomas saw it, was how to treat usurers and what to do with revenue that came from usury, not how to treat Jews as such. As Bernhard Blumenkranz has pointed out, an alternate title found on a few of the extant manuscripts, *De Regimine Subditorum*, gives a more accurate indication of the letter's contents.[54] Nevertheless, the letter does provide some important information about Aquinas's ideas on the economic and political status of Jews in a Christian society.

Thomas begins his letter by emphasizing his reluctance to reply to Marguerite's inquiries. For one thing, his work as a professor of theology at the University of Paris was keeping him very busy. More important, he did not feel he was fully qualified to deal with such issues. "I would have preferred you seek the advice of others who are more expert in such matters."[55] On one level, Aquinas's deference is extraordinary; in all his writings—which include works of philosophy, theology, and biblical exegesis as well as commentaries on Aristotle's cosmological and meteorological works, speculation on the biology of reproduction and fetal development, and a letter on the function of the heart—I know of no other occasion where Thomas confessed he was incompetent to deal with an issue. On another level, however, his remark makes sense. Essentially, he was telling Marguerite to go get herself a lawyer. The Countess was asking about precisely the sort of legal issues Aquinas avoids in the *Summa Theologiae*: What should be done with tax revenues whose source was usury? Is it licit to charge a fee for appointing someone to an administrative office? Under what conditions can new taxes be levied? For Aquinas, morality—his field of expertise—is concerned with general moral principles. Applying these principles to specific social and political questions is the job of legislators and lawyers. Laws are not deduced from moral precepts; rather, they require choices (*determinationes*) made in light of them. Once a law is established, however, rulers and subjects alike are obliged to follow it, unless there are very weighty reasons not to. Thus Thomas was telling Marguerite that these were legal issues, not moral questions, and as such they were outside his field. Her obligation was to obey the law, and a lawyer would serve better than he for finding out what the law required. Still, because of her kindness to his order, Aquinas agreed to respond to her inquiries.

The first question Marguerite had posed was whether Jews could be taxed at all.[56] Initially, the question seems curious. Why should Jews not be taxed like any other citizens? Marguerite, however, was proceeding from the medieval assumptions that princes and monarchs should "live of their own"; that is, they should rely on income generated by their personal estates or by traditional levies and privileges to support themselves. New taxes should be imposed only in extraordinary circumstances, not to support the day-to-day operations of court and government.[57] But Jews were a special case. Because they crucified Jesus and refuse to accept the Gospel, they are condemned to slavery. "Generally speaking, as the laws state, the Jews were, or are, condemned to perpetual slavery by merit of their guilt. Thus rulers may regard as their own whatever property Jews possess, as long as they allow them the means to remain alive."[58] In Aquinas's view, one consequence of Jewish servitude is that Jews may be taxed into destitution. But just because a ruler has the right to do something does not mean he should do it. Other considerations apply.

> Nevertheless, we must deal honestly even with those who are not under the spiritual authority of the Church,[59] lest the name of Christ be blasphemed, as the Apostle warns us by his own example, and act in such a way that no offense will be given to Jews or Gentiles or to the Church of God. This principle would seem to be best observed, as the laws indicate, by refraining from exacting forced services, which in past times were not customary, since what is unaccustomed is disturbing to people.[60]

As Thomas sees it, levying new taxes against the Jews might cause them to curse Christ or perceive Christians as unjust. Here again we see two recurrent features of Aquinas's social teaching: Concern for the Church's honor, and a profound conservatism that requires Jews continue to be treated as they have been in the past.

The other question posed by Marguerite that concerned Jews as such was whether they should be required to wear some sort of distinctive garb. In formulating his response, Aquinas turned again to the *Decretales*, this time explicitly citing the famous canon of the Fourth Lateran Council which required Jews and Moslems to dress in a manner that would make them easy to identify.

> The response to this question is clear, since, according to the statute of the general council, Jews of each sex in all Christian lands and at all times should

> be distinguished from other people by their dress. This is also required by their own law, which states that they should wear a four-cornered, fringed garment to enable others to recognize them.[61]

Here Thomas paraphrases the relevant canon. The only thing he adds is the mention of the specific garment Jews should wear; even in citing canon law the theology professor cannot resist appending a biblical footnote.

In dealing with Marguerite's queries regarding usury, however, Aquinas was not content simply to repeat legal precepts, for he saw this as a properly moral question. The Fourth Lateran Council and subsequent papal documents had commanded Jews to refrain from "heavy" or "immoderate" usury. On this issue, however, Aquinas was a zealot. As he made clear in the *Summa Theologiae*, he thought *all* usury was excessive: "Lending money at interest is intrinsically unjust."[62] He did acknowledge that civil law sometimes permitted usury, just as it often allowed prostitution. Given the imperfect nature of human society, he noted, arguing along Augustinian lines, more harm than good might result if government attempted to eradicate all immoral practices.[63] But in the *De Regimine Iudaeorum* Aquinas makes no such concessions to human imperfection. He declares that usury should be punished more harshly than other crimes, since it is manifest that usurers have no title to the money they possess; efforts must be made to return tax revenues exacted from usurers to the rightful owners; money from fines levied on usurers must be given to those who have been exploited by interest-bearing loans; gifts may be received from usurers, but these too must be transferred to fleeced borrowers. If the borrowers cannot be found, the money must be put to pious use according to the counsel of the diocesan bishop or other "upright men," or, if necessity warrants, used for the benefit of the community.

Aquinas's determination to be more Catholic than the pope on the question of usury reflects his moral passion on this issue. It is important to note, however, that it is the evil of usury which inspires this passion, not animus toward Jews as such. He twice notes that his strictures on usury apply to Christians as well as Jews.

> What has been said about Jews should also be understood to apply to Cahorsians and anyone else who persists in the evil practice of usury.[64]

> It seems to me that a Jew, or any other usurer, should be fined more heavily than others who are punished with fines, since they are known to have less title to the money taken from them.[65]

In sum, Aquinas's position on usury in the *De Regimine Iudaeorum* is much stricter than the one he adopts in the *Summa*. In his letter to Marguerite, Aquinas leaves no room for a prudential decision to allow usury in order to prevent greater evils; rather, he compares those who allow usury to negligent rulers who permit their subjects to practice fraud and piracy. Nor is the loss of revenue that would be suffered if the practice were stamped out a legitimate reason for permitting usurers to continue their spoilation.

> If it is objected that princes would suffer from such a policy, we must reply that they have brought this suffering on themselves. It would be better for them to compel Jews to work for a living, as is done in parts of Italy, than to allow them to live in idleness and grow rich by usury. If rulers suffer loss, it is only because they have been negligent.[66]

Though he speaks abstractly of "princes," Thomas's remarks are angry and reproachful. Perhaps he meant to reproach Marguerite for tolerating usury, but more likely he was expressing his disgust at those Christian rulers who winked at usury and used the taxes on its profits to fill their coffers. In any case, while Aquinas certainly thought Jewish usurers should be punished, he believed Christian usury was equally reprehensible, and he was also convinced that the ultimate responsibility for controlling it lay with secular rulers. It is also notable that he did not even hint at expelling Jews as a means of eliminating usury, though this was a tactic European rulers had used before and would soon turn to again.

6. Aquinas and the Persecution of European Jews

> Casum Iudaeorum esse miserandum, quia ex ignorantia peccaverunt . . . [sed] casus non est excusabilis ex toto, quia eorum ignorantia non fuit invincibilis vel ex necessitate existens, sed quodammodo voluntaria.
>
> —*Super Epistolam ad Romanos* 10.3

At the outset of this study, we posed three questions: What was Aquinas's attitude toward Judaism and the Jews? What were its social and theological sources? How did Aquinas contribute to medieval hostility and violence toward Jews? Having dealt with the first two questions in considerable detail, we are now in a position to turn to the third.

In true Thomistic fashion, we may begin with a distinction. First, to what extent did Aquinas's writings help entrench the hostility toward Jews that already existed? The answer should already be clear: because of his skill in explicating and rationalizing the traditional theological and canonistic attitude toward Jews, and because of his subsequent influence within the Dominican Order and on medieval thought generally, Aquinas did much to reinforce a status quo in which Jews were tolerated and allowed to worship but were subjected to a variety of discriminatory laws. Second, how did Thomas contribute to *innovative* types of hostility toward Jews? Here the answer is more complex.

Between 1096 and 1300, four fundamentally novel types of hostility toward Jews appeared: pogroms associated with the Crusades; violence stemming from paranoid beliefs that had little or no basis in fact, such as the myth that Jews crucified Christian children or desecrated the Eucharist; intrusive efforts to convert Jews to Christianity; and various fines, seizures of property, and expulsions based on the claim that all or most Jews in a given region were usurers.

The first two categories can be dispensed with quickly. Aquinas had nothing to do with the anti-Jewish violence that accompanied the Crusades or with executions and lynchings based on paranoid fantasies. He never mentioned the killing or forced conversion of Jews by Crusaders, but he was very clear in his teaching on killing and forced conversion in general: Except in the context of a just war or a judicial execution, Thomas thought all killing was immoral and should be punished, and he believed conversion should "in no way" be coerced. There is nothing in his moral doctrine that could serve to justify mob violence. Similarly, Aquinas did not comment on the belief that Jews killed and ate Christian children. Like Pope Gregory IX, however, he was well aware that murder and cannibalism were violations of Mosaic Law, and, as we have seen, he was convinced that medieval Jews generally observed the Law. The claim that Jews abused consecrated hosts was not heard until after Thomas's death, but it seems doubtful he would have given it much credence either since he knew that Jews did not believe in the efficacy of Christian sacraments. In any case, he certainly made no direct contribution to the development of these myths.

The relation of Aquinas's teaching to the innovative missionary techniques of Pablo Christiani and others is more nuanced. Christiani, like Raymond Marti, the author of the *Pugio Fidei*, was a member of the Order of Preachers, as was Aquinas. By itself, however, this means little. The Dominicans were a large and disparate order, and there is no evidence that Aquinas knew Christiani or Marti, though it seems likely he was at least aware of Christiani's presence in Paris in 1269, since he was there at the same time. More important, nothing in Aquinas's writings indicates that he thought the Talmud could be useful to Christian missionaries, and, as we have noted, when Raymond de Peñafort asked Thomas to compose a guide for missionaries, the work he produced, the *Summa Contra Gentiles*, relied solely on rational arguments to persuade Jews and Moslems of Christian truth; there is only a single, disparaging reference to the Talmud in the entire book. Hence there is no direct link between Aquinas and the "new missionizing."

Interestingly, however, some of the ideas about Judaism that underlie the Christiani/Marti approach are very similar to Thomistic doctrine. The project of using the Talmud to prove Jesus was the Messiah assumed that at least some of the Talmudic sages believed that Jesus was Christ. To Jews, of course, this notion was incomprehensible—as Nachmanides asked, if the sages believed this, why did they remain Jews?—but it does mesh with Aquinas's "malicious theory" of the Crucifixion, which asserts the priests and Pharisees knew Jesus was the Messiah but killed him anyway. Christiani and Marti also collapsed the distinction between Judaism and heresy. They argued that since authoritative Jewish texts gave witness to Jesus, faithful Jews had no choice but to accept Christianity. Aquinas, of course, did not make this move. In order to defend the Church's teaching and social practice, he was forced to make a sharp distinction between Judaism and heresy. But several elements of his theology pointed in another direction: his assertion that Jews who observed the Mosaic Law accepted the Gospel "in figura," his claim that first-century Jewish religious authorities had known Jesus was the Christ, and his argument that the Resurrection made the truth of Christianity manifest all tended to blur the line between Jews and heretical or apostate Christians. In sum, if Aquinas's ideas on Judaism were representative of mainstream thirteenth-century thought, it is easy to see how someone who shared those ideas but was less conservative than Aquinas, or was motivated by a particular animus toward Jews, might have concluded that Jews were heretics and should be treated as such.

Thus far, then, the connection between Aquinas and novel manifestations of hostility toward Jews is tenuous. Aquinas was firmly opposed to mob violence and forced conversions, and he lent no support to paranoid myths about Jews; at most, his ideas may have contributed to a cultural and theological milieu that made "innovative missionizing" and treating Jews as heretics possible. Even here, however, he did not play a direct role. Aquinas did not personally support the methods of Christiani and Marti, nor did he argue that Jews were heretics.

Only on the issue of usury did Aquinas's ideas represent a direct threat to the security of European Jews. In every other facet of his social teaching on Jews, Thomas firmly supported the principle of *Sicut Iudaeis*: Just as Jews should not be granted new privileges, neither should those they possess be taken from them. But usury was a different matter.

By 1270, lending money at interest had been considered a peculiarly Jewish activity for some two centuries. The princes and monarchs of western Europe had condoned, and sometimes encouraged, Jewish creditors; in many areas they used force to help them collect on bad loans. In 1215 the Fourth Lateran Council had denounced "excessive" usury, but the Church did not condemn all interest on loans, and it was well known that many popes borrowed from Jewish creditors. On the basis of this evidence, Aquinas could have invoked the notion of *consuetudo*—the process whereby custom acquires force of law—to conclude that the traditional tolerance of moneylending by Jews gave them a legal right to engage in this activity.[1] But he did not. Instead, he adopted an uncharacteristically radical position: All interest taking, he declared, was intrinsically unjust. In the *Summa Theologiae* he provided a loophole that could be used to justify permitting usury; as in the case of prostitution, he noted, it is sometimes prudent for rulers to allow minor evils in order to prevent greater ones. But when Marguerite wrote to ask him what she should do about Jewish usury, Aquinas was intransigent. Usury, he informed the countess in the *De Regimine Iudaeorum*, should be suppressed, and rulers who failed to do so were negligent.

It might be argued that the *Summa* reflects Aquinas's true thinking on the matter. The *secunda secundae* was composed a year or so after the *De Regimine Iudaeorum*, and in any case Aquinas's reply to Marguerite was merely an occasional letter in which he twice declared he was not an authority on the questions she had asked him. Be this as it may, the *De Regimine Iudaeorum* was probably at least as influential as the *Summa* on the development of Christian thought about usury in the period 1300–1500, and it was certainly much more prophetic. The letter was widely circulated: it survives in 83 manuscripts, an unusually large number for an *opusculum*.[2] Also, between 1450 and 1500, some nine early printed editions of the *De Regimine* were published.[3] Clearly Aquinas's little letter found an audience. It was popular not only because it called for the suppression of usury, but also because it provided a rationale for confiscating Jewish property: Thomas claimed rulers were obligated to seize funds obtained through usury and either return them to their rightful owners or use them for the good of the community. Knowingly or not, Aquinas had helped provide a moral figleaf for monarchs and princes who were only too anxious to enrich themselves and appear pious at the same time. In 1290, Edward I of England used the pretext of Jewish usury to confiscate their property and expel them from the kingdom; Philip IV did the same in France in 1306. Similar seizures and expulsions followed over the next three centuries. The city of Ulm, for instance, expelled its Jewish community in 1499. In the quarter-century prior to this expulsion, Ulm printers had published four editions of the *De Regimine Iudaeorum*.[4]

When the gap between theory and perceived reality becomes too great, something gives. By the early 1270s, when Aquinas wrote the *Summa Theologiae* and *De Regimine Iudaeorum*, such a gap had developed between the traditional policy of tolerating Jews and the social pressures opposed to that policy. First developed by Augustine and Pope Gregory the Great, the policy of limited toleration had remained intact—or rather had survived in dormant form—through some four centuries (c.600–1000) of Christian intellectual decline and missionary stasis. The revival of Christian learning, in the mid-eleventh century, led to the rediscovery and codification of this principle, and for more than two hundred years it stood virtually alone against a host of social, religious, and economic pressures that militated against European Jews. Modern historians, informed by the ideals of liberal tolerance, always feel compelled to explain instances of oppression and persecution, but in light of the treatment meted out to heretics and pagans in the Middle Ages, the long period in which Jews were tolerated in Christian Europe is at least as difficult to account for as their eventual expulsion.

Aquinas's social teaching on Jews is a good gauge of just how precarious the principle of toleration had become by 1270. His arguments for limited tolerance simply do not seem compelling within the framework of his own thought; he could have arrived at very different conclusions without violating a single major Thomistic principle. And toleration of Jews certainly did not flow logically from the theological vision embodied in canon law, which saw them as wicked, guilty, and intensely dangerous. The cornerstone of medieval toleration was the notion that it was somehow beneficial to Christians that Jews continue to exist in their midst. Aquinas and others continued to support this view, but in terms of social reality their arguments had ceased to make sense. While thirteenth-century Jews did not represent much of an objective threat to Christendom, it is hard to see how their presence contributed to its strength either.

Actually, the Augustinian rationale for tolerating Jews had been problematic from the start. Augustine had claimed that the existence of Jews helped convince pagans that Christians had not invented the prophecies of the Old Testament. But those same Jews who supposedly bore witness to Christianity were also quite capable of vigorously contesting the claim that Jesus of Nazareth had fulfilled the messianic prophecies. And by the thirteenth century, whatever plausibility the argument might have once had was largely dissipated, because by then Moslems and Jews—people who did not need to be convinced of the authority of such texts—were the primary target of Christian missionaries. Also, those pagans who were the object of proselytizing efforts, such as the Slavs on the eastern frontier of the Empire, were largely illiterate and hence not inclined to challenge the validity of the biblical canon. In sum, the Augustinian view, first formulated when the memory of imperial tolerance of Jews was fresh and when Christians were trying to convert literate pagans, had nothing to do with the goals and aspirations of thirteenth-century society. The literary Jews of the Old Testament were the only ones medieval Christians needed to give "witness" to their faith. Real Jews were merely a troublesome reminder that not everyone believed the truth of Catholic dogma was self-evident.

In the medieval context, Aquinas's attitude toward Jews was pedestrian, even banal. Though his education and talents enabled him to express them in an unusually clear and systematic way, his views essentially mirrored those of his era and his class. Thomas harbored no special malice toward Jews; he was not a Pablo Christiani or John of Capistrano, obsessed with converting Jews or whipping up popular enthusiasm against them. Even his demands that usury be suppressed were based on a moral conviction that usury was wrong rather than on any hatred of Jews as such. On most other issues—tolerating Jews, allowing them freedom of worship and the right to raise their children as they saw fit, while also discriminating against them and maintaining hedges against their influence—he was representative of an older tradition, a tradition rooted in *Sicut Iudaeis*, Gregory the Great, Augustine, and ultimately Paul. But by the late thirteenth century this tradition was largely out of touch with the forces of social change. With their aggressive self-confidence and secret insecurities, the leaders of Christian Europe were no longer content with the status quo. They accepted the stereotypes theologians such as Aquinas had helped develop and perpetuate—the image of Jews as dangerous infidels, as usurers, as Christ-killers—and acted on them by seeking to remove the Jews from their midst. In the face of such pressures, the more tolerant tradition that Thomas Aquinas represented was simply irrelevant.

Abbreviations

AH,*ST*	Alexandri de Hales, *Summa Theologica*, 4 vols. (Quaracchi: Collegium S. Bonaventurae, 1948).
ChJ	Solomon Grayzel, *The Church and the Jews in the Thirteenth Century, 1198–1254* (Philadelphia: Dropse College Press, 1933).
ChJ 2	Solomon Grayzel and Kenneth Stow, *The Church and the Jews in the Thirteenth Century, 1254–1314*, vol. 2 (New York and Detroit: Wayne State University Press, 1989).
FTD	James A. Weisheipl, O.P., *Friar Thomas D'Aquino* (Washington, D.C.: Catholic University Press, 1974).
Guide	Moses Maimonides, *The Guide of the Perplexed*, trans. by Shlomo Pines (Chicago: University of Chicago Press, 1963).
Novel	In the *Corpus iuris canonici*, ed. Aemilius Friedberg (Leipzig, 1879–81; repr. Graz, 1959).
PL	*Patrologia cursus completus . . . series Latina*, ed. J.-P. Migne, 221 vols. (Paris: J.-P. Migne, 1844–64).
SBMA	Berryl Smalley, *The Study of the Bible in the Middle Ages*, 3rd ed. (London: Oxford University Press, 1983).
SRH	Salo W. Baron, *A Social and Religious History of the Jews*, 2nd ed. 18 vols. (New York: Columbia University Press, 1952–83).
X	*Decretales* of Pope Gregory IX (*Liber Extra*), in the *Corpus iuris canonici*, ed. Aemilius Friedberg. (Leipzig, 1879–81; repr. Graz, 1959).

Works by Aquinas

Citations are to Thomas Aquinas, *Opera Omnia*, ed. Roberto Busa, 7 vols. (Holzboog: Friedrich Fromann, 1980). The specific works are abbreviated as follows:

CIS	*In Isaiam*
CPH	*In Hieremiam*

CRO	*Super Epistolam ad Romanos*
DRI	*De Regimine Iudaeorum*
QDL	*Quodlibeta*
QDM	*Quaestiones Disputata De Malo*
QDV	*Quaestiones Disputate De Veritate*
REI	*Super Evangelium Iohannis*
REM	*Super Evangelium Matthaei*
RGL	*Super Epistolam ad Galatas*
RHE	*Super Epistolam ad Hebraeos*
RPS	*In Psalmos*
R1C	*Super 1 Epistolam ad Corinthos*
SCG	*Summa Contra Gentiles*
ST1	*Summa Theologiae Prima Pars*
ST1–2	*Summa Theologiae Prima Secundae*
ST2–2	*Summa Theologiae Secunda Secundae*
ST3	*Summa Theologiae Tertia Pars*
1SN	*In 1 Sententiam*
2SN	*In 2 Sententiam*
3SN	*In 3 Sententiam*
4SN	*In 4 Sententiam*

Notes

Introduction

1. *Vatican Council II: The Conciliar and Post Conc]iliar Documents*, edited by Austin Flannery (Northport, N.Y.: Costello, 1975), 741.

2. H. Gayraud, *L'antisemitisme de S. Thomas d'Aquin* (Paris, 1896); S. Deploige, *S. Thomas et la question juive* (Louvain, 1897).

3. B. Mailloux, *S. Thomas et les Juifs* (Montreal, 1935). Though it has not focused on Aquinas, the scholarly controversy over "medieval antisemitism" has continued; Gavin Langmuir's *History, Religion, and Antisemitism* (Berkeley: University of California Press, 1990) is a recent contribution.

4. Alexander Broadie, "Medieval Jewry Through the Eyes of Aquinas," in *Aquinas and Problems of His Time*, ed. G. Verbeke and D. Verhelst (Louvain: Louvain University Press, 1976), 57–69, is essentially apologetic. Despite its title, Dieter Berg, "Servitus Iudaeorum. Zum Verhaltnis des Thomas von Aquin und seines Ordens zu den Juden in Europa im 13. Jahrhundert," in *Thomas von Aquin: Werk und Wirkung im Licht neuerer Forschungen*, ed. Albert Zimmerman (Berlin, 1988), actually says little specifically about Aquinas. More useful are Hans Liebeschutz, "Judaism and Jewry in the Social Doctrine of Thomas Aquinas," *Journal of Jewish Studies* 12 (1961): 57–81, and Bernhard Blumenkranz, "Le *De regimine Iudaeorum*: ses modeles, son exemple," in *Aquinas and Problems of His Time*, 101–17.

5. Jeremy Cohen, *The Friars and the Jews* (Ithaca, N.Y.: Cornell University Press, 1982).

6. Ibid., 13.

7. Robert Chazan, *Daggers of Faith* (Berkeley: University of California Press, 1989), 175–79.

Chapter 1

1. There is an enormous body of scholarship dealing with the question of Paul's attitude toward Jews and Judaism. For a good summary of the traditional view, see Rosemary Reuther, *Faith and Fratricide* (New York: Seabury Press, 1974), 96–107. Recently Lloyd Gaston and John Gager have offered a radical reinterpretation of Paul's doctrine, arguing that Paul viewed Christianity as a specifically gentile religion which supplemented but did not supersede or replace Judaism. See Lloyd Gaston, "Paul and the Torah," in *Anti-Semitism and the Foundations of Christianity*,

ed. Alan Davies (New York: Paulist Press, 1979), 48–71; and John Gager, *The Origins of Anti-Semitism* (London: Oxford University Press, 1985), 193–264. This view rests on the assumptions that Colossians and the Pastoral Epistles are non-Pauline and that the portrayal of Paul's views in Acts is misleading, as well as on a controversial reading of key passages in Romans. In any case, the Gaston/Gager thesis is irrelevant for the purposes of this book, since patristic and medieval theologians assumed the integrity and unity of the Pauline corpus.

2. The key texts are: Romans 2–4, 7, and 9–11; Galatians 2–5.12; Ephesians 2.11–22; Philippians 3.1–8; Colossians 2.10–15; 1 Timothy 1.8–11; and Acts 15.1–21.

3. For a summary of the patristic polemical literature, see A. Lukyn Williams, *Adversus Judaeos* (Cambridge: Cambridge University Press, 1935). Marcel Simon, *Verus Israel*, trans. H. McKeating (London: Oxford University Press, 1986), 135–233, analyzes patristic attitudes in the context of competition between Christianity and a vigorous, proselytizing Judaism. For an opposing view, see Edouard Will and Claude Orrieux, *Proselytisme juif?* (Paris: Belles Lettres, 1992).

4. More recently, some Augustine enthusiasts have claimed that *rationes seminales* were an anticipation of Darwin's theory of evolution.

5. Bernard Blumenkranz has analyzed these texts at length in his *Die Judenpredigt Augustins* (Basel: Helbing and Lichtenhahn, 1946); see also his "Augustin et les juifs; Augustin et le judaisme," *Recherches Augustiniennes* 1 (1958): 225–41.

6. *The City of God*, trans. Marcus Dods (New York: Random House, 1950), 18.45.

7. This idea is developed most fully in *The City of God* 18.45; see also Augustine's *Tractatus contra Iudaeos* 7.9 (*PL* 42, 57.)

8. *Tractatus contra Iudaeos* 10.1 (*PL* 42, 63–64).

9. Simon, 94, notes that the bitterest anti-Jewish polemics were produced in the East, where both Jewish proselytizing and judaizing tendencies among Christians were more common.

10. Simon, 177.

11. *SBMA*, 21.

12. *SBMA*, 124, 149–56.

13. See, for instance, *Epistle 121* (*PL* 22, 1006), *In Isaiam* 11.6 (*PL* 24, 150), *In Ezekiel* 38 (*PL* 25, 370).

14. *In Amos* 5.23 (*PL* 25, 1054). See also Simon, 216.

15. *FTD*, 121.

16. "His passion in the [anti-Jewish] cause, and the violence of his invective, are without parallel in the literature of the first few centuries," Simon, 222. Robert L. Wilken, *John Chrysostom and the Jews* (Berkeley: University of California Press, 1983), argues that Chrysostom's anti-Jewish polemics should be interpreted as a legitimate response, within Greek rhetorical conventions, to the danger Judaism and judaizing tendencies posed to Chrysostom's congregation in Antioch. He agrees however that, read in other contexts, Chrysostom's invective has done great harm.

17. Paul Harkins, ed., *Discourses Against Judaizing Christians* (Washington, D.C.: Catholic University Press, 1979).

18. Gregory the Great was another important influence. For his attitude toward Jews, see Chapter 2.

Chapter 2

1. Kenneth R. Stow, *Alienated Minority: The Jews of Medieval Latin Europe* (Cambridge, Mass.: Harvard University Press, 1992), 6–7; William C. Jordan, *The French Monarchy and the Jews* (Philadelphia: University of Pennsylvania Press, 1989), 48–61.

2. *SBMA*, 156–72.

3. Jordan, 11.

4. *SRH* IX, 59–60.

5. Apparently Bernard of Clairvaux, in the 1140s, was the first to use the verb *iudaizare* in this sense. See R. I. Moore, *The Formation of a Persecuting Society* (New York and Oxford: Basil Blackwell, 1987), 84.

6. For the French *captiones*, see Jordan, 66–69, 95–104, and 200–213. For other examples, especially in Germany, see *SRH* IX, 170–225.

7. Lester Little, *Religious Poverty and the Profit Economy in Medieval Europe* (Ithaca, N.Y.: Cornell University Press, 1978), 42–57.

8. Little, 44. For a general survey of the portrayal of Jews in medieval Christian art, see Bernhard Blumenkranz, *Le Juif medieval au miroir de l'art chretien* (Paris: Mouton, 1966).

9. R. W. Southern, *Western Society and the Church in the Middle Ages* (New York: Penguin, 1970), 100–133.

10. Solomon Grayzel, "The Jews and Roman Law," *Jewish Quarterly Review* 59 (1968): 93–117.

11. *Novel* 146.1. See Benjamin Z. Kedar, "Canon Law and the Burning of the Talmud," *Bulletin of Medieval Canon Law* 9 (1979): 79–82, and Edward A. Synan, *The Popes and the Jews in the Middle Ages* (New York: Seton Hall, 1965), 29.

12. Mansi, *Conciliorum omnium amplissima Collectio*, 31 volumes (Florence and Venice, 1795 and seq.), 2.14, par. 50.

13. Bernard Blumenkranz, *Juifs et chrétiens dans le monde occidental, 430–1096* (Paris: Mouton, 1960), 209–11.

14. On Agobard, see A. J. Zuckerman, "The Political Uses of Theology: The Conflict of Bishop Agobard and the Jews of Lyons", *Studies in Medieval Culture* 3 (1970): 23–51. For Leo VII, see his letter to the Archbishop of Mainz (*PL* 132, 1083).

15. For a description of Gregory's Jewish policy, see S. Katz, "Gregory the Great and the Jews," *Jewish Quarterly Review* 24 (1933–34): 113–36. B. Blumenkranz has collected the important texts: *Les Auteurs chrétiens latins du moyen âge sur les juifs et le judaisme* (Paris: Mouton, 1963), 73–86.

16. "Sicut Iudaeis non debet esse licentia quicquam in synagogis suis ultra quam permissum est lege praesumere, ita in his quae eis concessa sunt nullum debent praeiudicium sustinere." Shlomo Simonsohn, *The Apostolic See and the Jews: Documents, 492–1404* (Toronto: Pontifical Institute for Medieval Studies, 1988), 15.

17. Bernard Bachrach, *Early Medieval Jewish Policy in Western Europe* (Minneapolis: University of Minnesota Press, 1977).

18. Kenneth R. Stow, *The "1007 Anonymous" and Papal Sovereignty* (Cincinnati: Hebrew Union College and The Jewish Institute of Religion, 1984), 10.

19. "SICUT IUDAEIS non debet esse licentia in sinagogis suis, ultra quam permissum est, lege presumere, ita in hiis que concessa sunt nullum debent iudicium sustinere. Nos ergo, licet in sua magis velint duritia perdurare quam prophetarum verbo et suarum Scripturarum archana cognoscere atque ad christiane fidei et salutis notitiam pervenire; quia tamen defensionem nostram et auxilium postulant et christiane pietatis mansuetudinem . . . ipsorum petitionem admittimus, eisque protectionis nostre clipeum indulgemus.

"Statuimus etiam ut nullus christianus invitos vel nolentes eos ad baptismum per violentiam venire compellat; sed si eorum quilibet sponte ad christianos fidei causa confugerit, postquam voluntas eius fuerit patefacta, christianus absque aliqua efficiatur calumpnia; veram quippe christianitas fidem habere non creditur qui ad christianorum baptisma non spontaneus sed invitus congoscitur pervenire.

"Nullus etiam christianus eorum personas, sine iudicio potestatis, ferire, vulnerare aut occidere, vel suas illis pecunias auferre presumat, aut bonas, quas hactenus in ea quam habitant regione, habuerint consuetudines immutare.

"Preterea, in festivitatum suarum celebratione quisquam fustibus vel lapidibus eos ullatenus non perturbet; neque aliquis ab eis coacta servitia exigat, nisi ea que ipsi preteritis facere temporibus consuiverunt.

"Ad hec, malorum hominum pravitati et avaritie obviantes, decernimus ut nemo cimiterium judeorum mutilare vel minuere audeat, sive obtentu pecunie corpora humate effodere.

"Siquis autem decreti huius tenore cognito, temere quod absit, contraire temptaverit, honoris et officii sui periculum patiatur aut excommunicationis ultione plectatur, nisi presumptionem suam digna satisfactione correxerit. Eos autem dumtaxat huius protectionis presidio volumus communiri, qui nichil machinari presumpserint in subversionem fidei christiane."

There were variations in the text of *Sicut* each time it was issued. The version quoted here is that issued by Pope Alexander IV in 1255, found in *ChJ* 2, 2. For extended commentary on the bull, see Solomon Grayzel: "The Papal Bull *Sicut Iudeis*," in *Studies and Essays in Honor of Abraham A. Neuman*, ed. Meir Ben-Horin et al. (Philadelphia: Dropsie College Press, 1962), 243–80.

20. *ChJ*, 118.

21. "Mandamus quod Iudei capti huiusmodi occasione frivola a carcere liberentur nec deinceps huismodi occasione frivola capiantur, nisi forte, quod non credimus, in flagranti crimine caperentur." *ChJ* 2, 31.

22. Simonsohn, no. 373, 397–98.

23. "Iudei perfidi de cetero nullatenus insolescant sed sub timore servili pretendant semper verecundiam culpe sue, ac revereantur honorem fidei Christiane." From the bull *Etsi Iudeos*, in *ChJ*, 18.

24. In addition to the material contained in the two volumes of Solomon Grayzel's *The Church and the Jews in the Thirteenth Century*, see Simonsohn, *The*

Apostolic See and the Jews, for a collection of papal documents covering the entire Middle Ages.

25. "In diebus autem lamentationis dominice passionis, in publicum minime prodeant, eo quod nonnulli ex ipsis talibus diebus sicut accepimus ornatius non erubescunt incedere, ac Christianis, qui sacratissime passionis memoriam exhibentes, lamentationis signa pretendunt, illudere non formidant." *X* 5.10.5; *ChJ* 10.

26. Religious separatism, born of a desire to purify the faith and avoid syncretism or apostasy, was not an exclusively Christian phenomenon, of course; the Hasdai Ashkenaz and other Jewish rigorists often urged Jews to avoid unnecessary contacts with Christians. See Jacob Katz, *Exclusiveness and Tolerance* (London: Oxford University Press, 1963).

27. Kenneth Stow, "Papal and Royal Attitudes toward Jewish Lending in the Thirteenth Century," *Association for Jewish Studies Review*, 6 (1981): 161–83.

28. Solomon Grayzel, "Popes, Jews, and Inquisition from 'Sicut' to 'Turbato,'" in *Essays on the Occasion of the Seventieth Anniversary of Dropsie University*, ed. A. L. Katsch et al. (Philadelphia: Dropsie University Press, 1979), 164.

29. Daniel J. Silver, *Maimonidean Criticism and the Maimonidean Controversy, 1180–1240* (Leiden: E.J. Brill, 1965), 148–98.

30. See *ChJ* no. 95–96 and 119 for the relevant papal documents. Among the more recent discussions of Donin and the "Talmud Trial," see Robert Chazan, *Medieval Jewry in Northern France: A Political and Social History* (Baltimore and London: Johns Hopkins University Press, 1973), 124–33; Cohen, *The Friars and the Jews* (Ithaca, N.Y.: Cornell University Press, 1982), 61–76; Jordan, *French Monarchy*, 137–41.

31. *ChJ*, 119.

32. Solomon Grayzel, "The Talmud and the Medieval Papacy," in *Essays in Honor of Solomon B. Freehof*, ed. Walter Jacob et al. (Pittsburgh: Rodef Shalom Congregation, 1964), 220–45.

33. Robert Chazan has examined this "innovative argumentation" at length in *Daggers of Faith* (Berkeley: University of California Press, 1989). See also Cohen, *Friars*, 103–69; and Hyam Maccoby, *Judaism on Trial* (Rutherford, N.J.: Fairleigh Dickinson University Press, 1982), 39–75.

34. David Berger, "Mission to the Jews and Jewish-Christian Contacts in the Polemical Literature of the High Middle Ages," *American Historical Review* 91 (1986): 576–91. 35. The main sources on the texts used by Christiani and his method of argumentation are the two accounts of the Barcelona disputation of 1263: the "official" Latin account, and the Hebrew account composed by the Jewish disputant at Barcelona, Rabbi Moses ben Nachman (Nachmanides). For the Latin account, see Y. Baer, "The Disputations of R. Yechiel of Paris and Nachmanides," *Tarbiz* 2 (1931): 185–87. Nachmanides' *Vikuah* is reprinted in Charles B. Chavel, *Kitvei Rabbenu Mosheh ben Nahman*, vol. I (Jerusalem, 1963), 297–320. There are several English translations of both texts; the most recent is Maccoby, 102–46. On the disputation itself, in addition to the works by Cohen and Chazan cited above, see C. Roth, "The Disputation of Barcelona," *Harvard Theological Review* 43 (1950): 117–44; M. A. Cohen, "Reflections on the Text and Context of the

Disputation of Barcelona," *Hebrew Union College Annual* 35 (1964): 157–92; and R. Chazan, "The Barcelona 'Disputation' of 1263: Christian Missionizing and Jewish Response," *Speculum* 52 (1977): 824–42, and, most recently, Chazan, *Barcelona and Beyond* (Berkeley: University of California Press, 1992).

36. Chazan, *Daggers*, 165.

37. Chazan, *Daggers*, 84.

Chapter 3

1. See *CRO* 4.3 and *REM* 8.11.

2. *The City of God*, trans. Marcus Dods (New York: Random House, 1950), 2.21.; see *ST1–2* 105.2 and *RPS* 2.1.

3. See *ST1–2* 98.6 ad 2 and *RHE* 8.3.

4. "Illae quae in Veteri testamento promissa sunt temporaliter, intelligenda sunt spiritualiter." *RHE* 4.1.

5. "Populus Iudaeorum ad hoc electus erat a Deo, quod ex eo Christus nasceretur. Et ideo oportuit totum illius populi statum esse propheticum et figuralem . . . etiam bella et gesta illius popula exponuntur mystice; non autem bella vel gesta Assyriorum vel Romanorum." *ST1–2* 104.2 ad 2.

6. In *ST1–2* 103.3 Aquinas answers fourteen objections; in articles four and five there are ten each, followed by twelve in article six. In 105.2 there are twelve; in 105.3, six; in 105.4, nine.

7. Scholars have followed suit. Cardinal Cajetan, in his sixteenth-century commentary on the *Summa*, skimmed very lightly over the lengthier articles on the *lex vetus*. His commentary is included in the Leonine edition of the text: S. Thomae Aquinatis, *Opera Omnia*, vols. I–XII (Rome, 1888–1906). More recently, the volume of the Blackfriar's edition of the *Summa* devoted to the "Treatise on the Old Law" conspicuously lacks the detailed annotation and supplemental interpretive essays which make the other volumes so useful.

8. Beryl Smalley, "William of Auvergne, John of La Rochelle, and Thomas Aquinas on the Old Law," in *St. Thomas Aquinas Commemorative Studies*, ed. Armand Mauer et al. (Toronto: Pontifical Institute for Medieval Studies, 1974), 47.

9. See the structural comparison in Smalley, "Old Law," 57–59.

10. Aquinas uses a variety of terms to describe the three groups; in *CRO* 5.6 he calls them *duri*, *mediocres*, and *perfecti*. This analysis is not original with Thomas; see John of La Rochelle's similar schema: AH,*ST* Inq. IV, Q. 6, M. 2, c. 5.

11. "Quantum igitur ad duros lex fuit data in flagellum, et quantum ad praecepta moralia, ad quorum observantiam cogebantur per poenae comminationem . . . et caeremonialia, quae ideo sunt multiplicata, ne liceret eis diis alienis alium cultum superaddere. . . . Sed proficientibus qui dicuntur mediocres, lex fuit in paedagogum . . . et hoc quantum ad caeremonialia, quibus continebantur in divino cultu, et quantum ad moralia, quibus ad iustitiam promovebantur. . . . Perfectis autem fuit quantum ad caeremonialia quidem in signum . . . quantum ad moralia vero in solatium . . ." *CRO* 5.6.

12. "De duobus enim homo superbiebat: scilicet de scientia et de potentia. De scientia quidem, quasi ratio naturalis ei posset sufficere ad salutem . . . et experimento homo discere potuit quod patiebatur rationis defectum, per hoc quod homines usque ad idolatriam et turpissima vitia. . . . Et ideo post haec tempora fuit necessarium legem scriptam dari in remedium humanae ignorantiae. . . . Sed postquam homo est instructus per legem, convicta est eius superbia de infirmitate, dum implere non poterat quod cognoscebat." *ST1–2* 98.6.

13. *CRO* 7.2.

14. *CRO* 7.2 and 4.2; see also *ST1–2* 98.1 ad 2.

15. "Illud quod subiacet hominis potestati, non reputat aliquis pro magno, sed illud quod est extra hominis potestatem, apprehenditur ab homine quasi magnum. Prohibitio autem eius quod concupiscitur ponit illud quod prohibetur quasi extra hominis potestatem, et ideo concupiscentia magis exardescit in rem concupitiam dum prohibetur. Secunda ratio est qui interiores affectiones quando interius retinentur, ita quod exterius non deriventur, ex hoc ipso magis interius incenduntur; sicut patet in dolore et ira, quae dum interius clause tenentur, magis augentur; si autem exterius quoquo modo procedant eorum virtus diminuitur. Prohibitio autem propter timorem poenae cogit hominem ut concupiscentiam suam ad exterior non perducat et ideo ipsa concupiscentia, interius retenta, magis inflammatur. Tertia ratio est, quia illud quod non est nobis prohibitum, apprehendimus quasi possibile fieri quandocumque nobis placuerit; et ideo multoties, opportunitate existente, illud vitamus; sed quando aliquid est prohibitum, apprehenditur a nobis, ut non semper a nobis haberi possit; et ideo quando opportunitas datur sine timore poenae illud consequendi, promptiores ad hos sumus." *CRO* 4.6.

16. Smalley, "Old Law," 28.

17. *ST1–2* 99.1.

18. "Omnia praecepta legis veteris sunt unum secundum ordinem ad unum finem; sunt tamen multa secundum diversitatem eorum quae ordinantur ad finem illum." *ST1–2* 99.1. Aquinas responded similarly to a query concerning the unity of natural law; see *ST1–2* 94.2.

19. *ST1–2* 99.2–4; see also *CRO* 2.4 and *RHE* 7.3. Note how close Thomas is to Maimonides here. Maimonides also held that the ultimate purpose of the Law was to lead man to communion with God, and that three proximate goals had to be attained for this to occur: humans had to learn justice, moral virtue, and religious truth.

"The true Law then . . . has come to bring us both perfections, I mean the welfare of the states of people in their relations with one another through the abolition of reciprocal wrongdoing and through the acquisition of a noble and excellent character. In this way the preservation of the population of the country and their permanent existence in the same order became possible, so that every one of them achieves his first perfection; I mean also the soundness of the beliefs and the giving of correct opinions through which ultimate perfection is achieved." *Guide* 3.27.

20. None of these terms has an exact English equivalent. *Moralia* prescribes general duties toward God as well as human persons. *Caeremonialia* includes dietary and cleanliness laws in addition to statutes pertaining directly to worship. *Iudicia-*

lia is especially complex; Aquinas uses it to indicate everything from political and constitutional ordinances to criminal law and civil procedure. See *ST1–2* 99.2–6; 100.1–2; 101.1–4; 104.1–4.

21. "A paucis, et per longum tempus, et cum admixtione multorum errorum." *ST1* 1.1 See also *ST1–2* 99.2 ad 2.

22. *ST1–2* 103.1.

23. *ST1–2* 99.3; 101.1–2.

24. *ST1–2* 99.4; 104.1.

25. "Nam praecepta primae tabulae, quae ordinant ad Deum, continent ipsum ordinem ad bonum commune et finale, quod Deus est; praecepta autem secundae tabulae continent ipsum ordinem iustitiae inter homines observandae, ut scilicet nulli fiat indebitum, et cuilibet reddatur debitum; secundum hanc enim rationem sunt intelligenda praecepta decalogi. Et ideo praecepta decalogi sunt omnino indispensabilia." *ST1–2* 100.8. By the "first tablet" Aquinas means the first three commandments; the remaining seven constitute the "second tablet". Though Thomas here refers specifically to the Decalogue, he makes it clear in 100.11 that the other moral precepts of the Mosaic Law are also part of the *lex naturalis*.

26. Note here the contrast with John of La Rochelle, who thought many Mosaic moral commandments were inadequate and had to be corrected by Christ's teaching. *AH*,ST Pars II Inq. IV Tract. I Q. VI a. 1 (n. 553).

27. This does not mean Aquinas thought every moral commandment in the Pentateuch was permanently valid. He believed the Decalogue contains universally valid moral *principles*, but he recognized that the Law also contains more specific precepts that could potentially be abrogated under certain circumstances. For the distinction between moral principles and more specific precepts, see below, 47–48.

28. "Praecepta legis naturae hoc modo se habent ad rationem practicam, sicut principia prima demonstrationem se habent ad rationem speculativam: utraque enim sunt quaedam principia per se nota." *ST1–2* 94.2.

29. "Bonum est faciendum et persequendum, et malum vitandum." *ST1–2* 94.2.

30. See *ST1–2* 94.4, 6; 100.1–2, 11. Aquinas's terminology is maddeningly inconsistent: in 94.4 he speaks of "prima principia" and "propria"; in 94.6 he uses "praecepta communissima" and "praecepta secundaria"; in 100.1 "communia et prima principia," others grasped "cum modica consideratione," and the third type that requires "multa conderatio diversarum circumstantiarum" to be understood; in 100.11 the categories are "certissima," "magis determinata," and "quaedam . . . quorum ratio non est adeo cuilibet manifesta." Thomas is also notoriously vague on precisely what is included in each category of precepts; for instance, it is difficult to reconcile the account in 94.2 based on human needs and inclinations with 100.3 ad 1 and 100.11, which speak of love of God and neighbor as "prima et communia praecepta legis naturae." Nevertheless, the basic three-tiered structure is clear. My account takes 94.4 and 100.11 as primary. Aquinas's theory of natural law has produced an enormous secondary literature. A good place to start is Germaine Grisez, "The First Principle of Practical Reason: A Commentary on *Summa Theologiae* 1–2, Question 94, Article 2," in *Aquinas: A Collection of Critical Essays*, ed. Anthony Kenny (Garden City, N.Y.: Anchor Books, 1969), 340–82.

31. *ST1–2* 100.3 ad 1; 100.11; 94.4.

32. *ST1–2* 94.6.

33. "In paucioribus circa huiusmodi contingit iudicium humanum perverti, huiusmodi editione indigent." *ST1–2* 100.11.

34. *ST1–2* 94.4.

35. "Quaedam vero sunt magis determinata . . . et haec sunt praecepta decalogi. Quaedam vero sunt quorum ratio non est adeo cuilibet manifesta, sed solum sapientibus: et ista sunt praecepta moralia superaddita decalogo, tradita a Deo populo per Moysen et Aaron." *ST1–2* 100.11.

36. *ST1–2* 100.11. Though in his own work Aquinas used the virtues rather than the Decalogue to structure his discussion of morality, his remarks here indicate he was not opposed in principle to schemes based on the Ten Commandments, which were much favored by the Franciscans and, later, the Jesuits.

37. "Praeceptum de observatione sabbati est secundum aliquid morale, inquantum scilicet per hoc praecipitur quod homo aliquo tempore vacet rebus divinis. . . . Et secundum hoc, inter praecepta decalogi computatur. Non autem quantum ad taxationem temporis: quia secundum hoc est caeremoniale." *ST1–2* 100.3 ad 2. Bonaventure made a similar distinction between the Sabbath commandment's moral and ceremonial elements. See Gilbert Dahan, "Saint Bonaventure et les Juifs," *Archivum Franciscanum Historicum* 77 (1984): 394–95.

38. *ST1–2* 100.1.

39. "Intentio legis divinae est ut constituat principaliter amicitiam hominium ad Deum. Cum autem similitudo sit ratio amoris . . . impossibile est esse amicitiam hominis ad Deum, qui est optimus, nisi homines boni efficiantur. . . . Et ideo oportuit praecepta legis veteris etiam de actibus virtutum dari. Et haec sunt moralis legis praecepta." *ST1–2* 99.2.

40. "Sicut Augustinus probat in libro *De spiritu et littera*, etiam littera legis quantum ad praecepta moralia, occidere dicitur occasionaliter; inquantum scilicet praecipit quod bonum est, non praebens auxilium gratiae ad implendum." *ST1–2* 99.2 ad 3. See also *CRO* 7.2, where Aquinas expands on this theme.

41. *ST1–2* 100.12.

42. "Ordinatur autem homo in Deum non solum per interiores actus mentis, qui sunt credere, sperare et amare; sed etiam per quaedam exteriora opera, quibus homo divinam servitutem profitetur." *ST1–2* 99.3.

43. "Rationes praeceptorum caeremonialium veteris legis dupliciter accipi possunt. Uno modo, ex ratione cultus divini qui erat pro tempore illo observandus. Et rationes istae sunt litterales: sive pertineant ad vitandum idololatriae cultum, sive ad rememoranda aliqua Dei beneficia, sive ad insinuandam excellentiam divinam, vel etiam ad designandam dispositionem mentis quae tunc requirebatur in colentibus Deum. Alio modo possunt eorum rationes assignari secundum quod ordinantur ad figurandum Christum. Et sic habent rationes figurales et mysticas: sive accipiantur ex ipso Christo et Ecclesia, quod pertinet all allegoriam; sive mores populi Christiani, quod pertinet ad moralitatem; sive ad statum futurae gloriae, prout in eam introducimur per Christum, quod pertinet ad anagogiam." *ST1–2* 102.2.

44. *ST1–2* 101.1 obj. 4.; see *Guide* 3.20.

45. "Ratio caeremonialium est quodammodo probabilis, non quod ex eo dicuntur caeremonialia quia eorum ratio non est manifest; sed hoc est quoddam consequens. Quia enim praecepta ad cultum Dei pertinentia oportet esse figuralia . . . inde est quod eorum ratio non est adeo manifesta." *ST1–2* 101.1 ad 4.

46. *ST1–2* 102.1 ad 3.

47. "Praecepta caeremonialia sunt figuralia primo et per se, tanquam instituta principaliter ad figurandum Christi mysteria et futura." *ST1–2* 104.3.

48. *ST1–2* 101.4.

49. *ST1–2* 102.3–6.

50. "Dicendum quod, etsi haedus occisus non sentiat qualiter carnes eius coquantur, tamen in animo decoquentis ad quandam crudelitatem pertinere videtur si lac matris, quod datum est ei pro nutrimento, adhibeatur ad consumptionem carnium ipsius. Vel potest dici quod gentiles in solemnitatibus idolorum taliter carnes haedi coquebant, ad immolandum vel ad comedendum. . . . Figuralis autem ratio huius prohibitionis est quia praefigurabatur quod Christus, qui est haedus propter 'similitudinem carnis peccate' (Rm. 8.3), non erat a Iudaeis coquendus, idest occidendus, in lacte matris, idest tempore infantiae. Vel significatur quod haedus, idest peccator, non est coquendus in lacte matris, idest non est blanditiis deliniendus." *ST1–2* 102.6 ad 4.

51. *SBMA*, 303.

52. "Litteralis ratio circumcisionis principalis quidem fuit ad protestationem fidei unius Dei. Et quia Abraham fuit primus qui se ab infidelibus separavit . . . ideo ipse primus circumcisionem accepit. . . . Et ut haec protestatio, et imitatio fidei Abrahae, firmaretur in cordibus Iudaeorum, acceperunt signum in carne sua, cuius oblivisci non possent. . . . Ideo autem fiebat octava die, quia antea puer est valde tenullus, et posset ex hoc graviter laedi. . . . Ideo vero non magis tardabatur, ne propter dolorem aliqui signum circumcisionis refugerent: et ne parentes etiam, quorum amor increscit ad filios post frequentem conversationem et eorum augmentum, eos circumcisioni subtraherent. Secunda ratio esse potuit ad debilitationem concupiscentiae in membro illo. Tertia ratio, in sugillationem cacrorum Veneris et Priapi, in quibus illa pars corporis honorabatur. . . . Figuralis vero ratio circumcisionis erat qui figurabatur ablatio corruptionis fienda per Christum, quae perfecte complebitur in octave aetate, quae est aetas resurgentium." *ST1–2* 102.5 ad 1.

53. See *Guide* 3.49.

54. *Guide 3.49*. Aquinas's entire analysis of the literal reasons for circumcision follows Maimonides very closely; only the connection with forbidding idolatry is original with Thomas, and even here he was simply applying a Maimonidean principle. Though Aquinas does occasionally cite Maimonides ("Rabbi Moyses") in his discussion of the *caeremonialia*, he often borrows without acknowledgment, as in this case.

55. J. Huizinga, *The Waning of the Middle Ages* (New York: Doubleday, 1954), 205–6.

56. *ST1–2* 102.5 ad 4 and 8 are especially striking examples of Thomas's typology run amok. Here and elsewhere, the *Glossa ordinaria* on Leviticus was his main source of traditional, symbolic exegesis. The *Glossa* in turn relied heavily on Origen and Gregory the Great. See Smalley, "Old Law," 12–13.

57. "Quia mysterium incarnationis et passionis Christi nondum erat realiter peractum, illae veteris legis ceremoniae non poterant in se continere realiter virtutem profluentem a Christo incarnato et passo, sicut continent sacramenta novae legis. . . . Poterat autem mens fidelium, tempore legis, per fidem coniungi Christo incarnato et passo: et ita ex fide Christi iustificabantur. Cuius fidei quaedam protestatio erat huiusmodi caeremoniarum observatio, inquantum erant figura Christi. Et ideo pro peccatis offerebantur sacrificia quaedam in veteri lege, non quia ipsa sacrificia a peccato emundarent, sed quia erant quaedam protestationes fidei, quae a peccato mundabat." *ST1–2* 103.2. See also *CRO* 4.2.

58. "Quamvis autem sit eadem fides quam habemus de Christo, et quam antiqui Patres habuerunt; tamen quia ipsi praecesserunt Christum, nos autem sequimur, eadem fides diversis verbis significatur a nobis et ab eis." *ST1–2* 103.4. See also *QDV* 14.11.

59. "Post peccatum [originale] autem fuit explicite creditum mysterium Christi non solum quantum ad incarnationem, sed etiam quantum ad passionem et resurrectionem, quibus humanum genus a peccato et morte liberatur." *ST2–2* 2.7.

60. *ST1–2* 102.4 ad 4.

61. *ST2–2* 2.7.

62. *RHE* 9.2.

63. Smalley, "Old Law," 17.

64. AH,*ST* Pars. II, Inq. III, Tract. 2, Sect. 2.

65. Maimonides has little to say about the political provisions of the Law; see *Guide* 3.39–42. John uses the *iudicialia* as an occasion to launch an extended discussion of statute law, procedure, and judging; AH,*ST* Pars. II, Inq. III, Tract. 2, Sect. 2, Q. 1. It seems likely that Aquinas had John's narrower understanding of the *iudicialia* in mind in the following reply to an objection: "Dicendum quod iudicia exercentur officio aliquorum principum, qui habent potestatem iudicandi. Ad principem autem pertinet non solum ordinare de his quae veniunt in litigium, sed etiam de voluntariis contractibus qui inter homines fiunt, et de omnibus pertinentibus ad populi communitatem et regimen. Unde praecepta iudicialia non solum sunt illa quae pertinent ad lites iudiciorum, sed etiam quaecumque pertinent ad ordinationem hominum ad invicem, quae subest ordinationi principis tanquam supremi iudicis." *ST1–2* 104.1 ad 1

66. *ST1–2* 105.2.

67. *ST1–2* 105.3.

68. "Quia filii Israel erant a Domino de servitute liberati, et per hoc divinae servituti addicti, noluit Dominus ut in perpetuum servi essent . . . ideo, quia simpliciter servi non erant, sed secundum quid, finito tempore, dimittebantur liberi." *ST1–2* 105.4 ad 1.

69. "Unum est ut omnes aliquam partem habeant in principatu: per hoc enim conservatur pax populi, et omnes talem ordinationem amant et custodiunt, ut dicitur in II Polit. Aliud est quod attenditur secundum speciem regiminis, vel ordinationis principatuum." *ST1–2* 105.1. The reference is to *Politics* 2.6 $1270^{b}17$.

70. "Moyses et eius successores gubernabant populum quasi singulariter omnibus principantes, quod est quaedam species regni. Eligebantur autem septuagina duo seniores secundum virtutem . . . et hoc erat aristocraticum. Sed demo-

craticum erat quod isti de omni populo eligebantur . . . et etiam quod populus eos eligebat. . . . Unde patet quod optima fuit ordinatio principum quam lex instituit." *ST*1–2 105.1. Aquinas's comments here have implications for his own political views. He even exaggerates the democratic element of the Mosaic polity; the elders were actually appointed by Moses, not elected by the people (Ex. 18.13–26). Contemporary readers could not have missed the implicit criticism of medieval kingship and the landed nobility; the article as a whole reads like an endorsement of the republican polity of some Italian city-states. Compare Aquinas's *De Regimine Principium* where, writing to a hereditary monarch, he does not reveal his preference for participatory government.

71. *ST*1–2 99.4

72. *ST*1–2 104.1.

73. "Populus Iudaeorum ad hoc electus erat a Deo, quod ex eo Christus nasceretur. Et ideo oportuit totum illius populi statum esse propheticum et figuralem." *ST*1–2 104.2 ad 2.

74. "Ad ordinandum statum illius populi secundum iustitiam et aequitatem." *ST*1–2 104.2.

75. See James Weisheipl's review of the Leonine edition of this commentary in *The Thomist* 43 (1979): 331–36.

76. "Potest ergo quadruplex tempus distingui. Primum ante legem scriptam et idolatriam: et tunc placebant antiqua sacrificia facta a sanctis patribus, et propter devotionem offerentis et propter significationem rei oblate. Secundum tempus est sub lege scripta: et tunc interveniente idolatria, additum fuit quiddam propter quod simpliciter displicebant, quia non erat dignum quod eodem placaretur Deus et coleretur diabolus; et ex alia parte fuit addita una utilitas ex parte offerentis, ut esset remedium contra idolatriam populo ad hoc prono: unde etiam de sacrificiis nichil preceptum est ante fabricationem idoli. . . . Tertium tempus fuit sub prophetis, in quo propter peccata populi iam non placebant ex parte offerentis, sed tantum in quantum erant signa: unde secundum hoc non placabant Deum sed magis offendebant. Quartum tempus est sub gratia, quando iam usus eorum ex toto abolitus est, quia veniente veritate cessavit figura." *CIS* 1.13.

77. See, inter alia, *CIS* 1.5, 5.7, 5.8, 5.17, 9.18–21; *CPH* 7.3, 17.4; *REI* 2.1.

78. *REM* 12.4.

79. *CRO* 2.4; see also *REI* 4.3.

80. See Chapter 4 for a detailed discussion of Aquinas's views on first-century Jewish society.

81. *RHE* 1.1.

Chapter 4

1. *FTD*, 360–73. The *Lectures on Matthew* were long thought to be among Aquinas's early works, but H. V. Schooner has demonstrated that Thomas delivered these lectures sometime after 1263, and very likely between 1269 and 1272: "La *Lectura super Matthaeum* V, 20–48 de Thomas d'Aquin," *Recherches de théologie ancienne et medievale*, 50 (1983), 145–90.

2. See for example *REI* 7.32, 11.45–48, 19.6–39; *REM* 15.1–20. This division was traditional in patristic and medieval exegesis.

3. Aquinas also mentions the Sadducees as the Jewish *secta* that did not believe in the resurrection. Generally, however, when he speaks of the *majores* or *principes* it is clear he has the Pharisees and Temple priests in mind. In this he simply follows the Gospels, where the Pharisees and priests are depicted as *the* leaders, with the Sadducees making only an occasional appearance.

4. According to Aquinas, when Jesus cast out the legion of demons into the herd of swine, he could not have been in Judea, since keeping pigs was forbidden by the Law; *REM* 8.31. Concerning the moneychangers in the temple, he remarks that though they were motivated by greed, "usuram inde non reciperent, quia hoc erat in lege prohibitum." *REI* 2.2.

5. "Gentiles perfectius et securius salutem consequebantur sub observantiis legis quam sub sola lege naturali." *ST1–2* 98.5 ad 3.

6. "Judaei per legem et prophetas veram cognitionem seu aestimationem de Deo habebant, in hoc quod non credebant ipsum esse corporeum, nec in uno loco determinato esse. . . . Nec etiam idola colebant. . . . Ideo vera notitia de Deo habebatur solum a Iudaeis". *REI* 4.2.

7. "Multi Iudaeorum erant iam dispositi per fidem." *REM* 10.5.

8. "Quia opinio eorum [erat] magis propinqua veritati, ideo Nicodemus facilius conversus est ad Christum." *REI* 3.1.

9. "A principio namque licet Dominus non elegerit sapientes, potentes aut nobiles, ne virtus fidei sapientiae et potentiae humanae attribueretur . . . voluit tamen aliquos sapientes et potentes a principio ad se convertere, ne si doctrina sua solum ab ignobilibus et insipientibus reciperetur, haberatur contemptui; et ne credentium multitudo potius attribueretur rusticitati et insipientiae conversorum, quam virtuti fidei." *REI* 3.1.

10. *REI* 8.4.

11. "Cold from lack of charity, but burning with desire to do evil, stealthily they draw near to harm, surrounding and squeezing, tormenting the soul." *REI* 10.5.

12. See *REI* 8.7, 10.3.

13. "Videntes miracula quae Christus faciebat, inducebantur ad fidem eius. Sed tamen fides eorum infirma erat, quia non a doctrina, sed a signis moventur ad credendum ei . . . [et] non credebant in Christum sicut in Deum, sed sicut in aliquem justum virum, seu prophetam." *REI* 7.5.

14. "Eius sermones transcendentes capacitatem humanam . . . [et quia] consuetudo rudium est, quod cum talia audiunt, diabolica reputant, credebant quod Christus quasi daemonio plenus loqueretur." *REI* 8.7.

15. "Pharisaei magis conveniebant nobiscum in opinionibus, qui credebant resurrectionem futuram, et dicebant esse creaturas aliquas spirituales . . . [et] opinio eorum probabilior erat, et magis propinqua veritati." *REI* 3.1.

16. "Duplex autem causa assignari potest quare Judaei hoc Christo dicebant. Una quidem, quia Samaritani gens odiosa erat pro populo Israelitico, eo quod decem tribubus in captivitatem ductis, terram eorum possidebant. . . . Quia ergo Christus Iudaeos arguens, credebatur a Iudaeis quod hoc ex odio faceret, ideo

eum Samaritanum et quasi adversarium reputabant etc. Alia ratio, quia Samaritani partim quidem servabant ritus Iudaicos, partim vero non. Videntes ergo Iudaei Christum in aliquo lègem servantem, et in aliquo dissolventem, utpote sabbatum, vocabant eum Samaritanum." *REI* 8.7.

17. *REM* 26.26.

18. In *REM* 15.9, Aquinas specifically identifies the Church's canon law as "human tradition."

19. For Thomas, applying law to specific situations is a matter for prudential choice, not logical deduction. In his view, the Pharisees' error was to claim that their decisions—many of which were just in themselves—were absolutely mandated by the Law. "In multis [observentiis] bene dicebant; tamen deficiebant, quia, ut dicitur, omnia provenire ex necessitate ponebant." *REM* 3.7.

20. *ST1–2* 19.1–4.

21. *REI* 11.7.

22. *REI* 11.7.

23. "Dicimus simpliciter concedendum esse quod Deus voluit Christum pati, mori, quia eius passio bonum fuit et causa nostrae salutis. Cum autem dicitur: 'Volebat eum pati vel occidi a Iudaeis,' hic distinguendum est. Si enim intelligitur sic: Volebat eum sustinere passionem sive crucifixionem a Iudaeis illatam, verus est sensus. Si vero intelligitur sic: Volebat ut Iudaei occiderent eum, falsum est; non enim volebat Deus actionem Iudaeorum, quae mala erat, sed volebat passionem bonam, et haec voluntas per malas Iudaeorum voluntates impleta est. Peter Lombard, *Sententiae in IV Libris Distinctae* (Rome, 1971), Liber I, Dist. XLVIII, Cap. 2. Dante presents this same distinction as a revelation given by Beatrice to the Pilgrim; see *Paradiso* 7.46–51.

24. "Deus Pater fuit causa efficiens mortis Christi, ut permittens et ut non prohibens mortem, cum posset; Christus vero ut passionem voluntarie suscipiens nec prohibens, cum posset; Iudaei vero et Iudas ut causa procurans; crucifixores vero ut causa inferens mortem." AH,*ST* Inq. I, Tract. V, Q. 1, Memb. VI, c. 2 ad 3 (n. 162).

25. "Christus voluit quidem suam passionem, sicut et Deus eam voluit; iniquam tamen actionem Iudaeorum noluit." *ST3* 47.6 ad 3. See also *3SN* 20.1.2 ad 3 and *QDM* 2.5 ad 10.

26. *ST3* 47.1.

27. "Eadem actio diversimode iudicatur in bono vel in malo, secundum quod ex diversa radice procedit. Pater enim tradidit Christum, et ipse seipsum, ex charitate; et ideo laudantur. Iudas autem tradidit ipsum ex cupiditate, Iudaei ex invidia, Pilatus ex timore mundano, quo timuit Caesarem; et ideo ipsi vituperantur." *ST3* 47.3 ad 3. Bonaventure also stressed the difference between the Crucifixion as a physical phenomenon and the intentions of the various agents, using the *opus operatum/opus operans* distinction favored by Franciscan theologians. See Gilbert Dahan, "Saint Bonaventure et les Juifs," *Archivum Franciscanum Historicum* 77 (1984): 397–98.

28. *ST3* 47.6 ad 2.

29. See *ST1–2* 18–21.

30. Translations of scripture are from the Vulgate.

31. For a survey of the western interpretation of these passages, see Jeremy Cohen, "The Jews as the Killers of Christ in the Latin Tradition from Augustine to the Friars," *Traditio* 39 (1983): 1–27.

32. *PL* 92.616.

33. Cohen, "The Jews as Killers of Christ," 11–12.

34. Aquinas was also aware of a passage in the *Opus Imperfectum in Mattheum*—a work which he, like everyone else at the time, thought was by John Chrysostom—indicating the Jewish leaders knew Jesus was divine; see *ST3* 47.5 ad 1.

35. "Sciendum tamen quod eorum ignorantia non eos excusabat a crimine: quia erat quodammodo ignorantia affectata. Videbant enim evidentia signa ipsius divinitatis: sed ex odio et invidia Christi ea pervertabant, et verbis eius, quibus se Dei Filium fatebatur, credere noluerunt." *ST3* 47.5.

36. "Ignorantia affectata non excusat a culpa, sed magis videtur culpam aggravare: ostendit enim hominem sic vehementer esse affectum ad peccandum quod vult ignorantiam incurrere ne peccatum vitet. Et ideo Iudaei peccaverunt, non solum hominis Christi, sed tanquam Dei crucifixores." *ST3* 47.5 ad 3.

Aquinas arrived at this conclusion sometime between 1256 and 1273. In his *Commentary on the Sentences* (1252–1256), he argued simply that those who killed Christ did not know he was divine, and that this mitigated their guilt. See *3SN* 19.1.2 ad 5. He considered the question at length in his commentary on I Corinthians 2.8, which was probably written between 1269 and 1272, one to four years before the third part of the *Summa*. Here he says that the Jewish *principes* did not know Jesus was divine because their vision was clouded by their envy and hatred of him, but he does not call this ignorance *ignorantia affectata* or indicate it exacerbated their guilt. See *R1C* 2.2. He says much the same thing in the *Commentary on John*, written about the same time, but adds that the ignorance of the Jewish leaders stemmed *ex certa malitia*: *REI* 15.5. Thus Thomas seems to have gradually developed his "malicious theory" of the Crucifixion. I suspect that his attitude toward Jews hardened in the 1260s under the influence of the enormous amount of Greek theology he read in preparation for writing the *Catena Aurea* and *Contra Errores Graecorum*. Unfortunately, because Aquinas wrote so little on Jews prior to 1260, it is impossible to test this hypothesis.

37. *ST1* 114.4.

38. *REI* 8.8.

39. *Ex certa malitia* can be roughly translated as "with knowing malice." To sin *ex certa malitia* means knowing that what you are doing is gravely wrong, and doing it anyway. According to Thomas, the Jews also sinned *ex certa malitia* when they accused Jesus of performing his miracles by using demonic powers. This sin, in his view, involved blasphemy against the Holy Spirit, and as such was unforgivable: *QDL* 2.8.1. Though he says here it was "the Jews" who did this, he must mean the *principes*, since only they had the knowledge that would have made it possible for the sin to be *ex certa malitia*.

40. A generation or so after Thomas, Duns Scotus and Nicholas of Lyra solved this particular problem by claiming that *all* first-century Jews had known Jesus was Messiah and Son of God; see Cohen, "The Jews as Killers of Christ," 20.

41. "Ideo magis peccaverunt, quia mirabilia viderunt, et tamen non crediderunt posses resurgere." *REM* 27.64.

42. *REI* 12.7.

43. "Post mortem Christ multi ingressi sunt Ecclesiam, ut caperent et insidiarentur sanctis viris." *RPS* 40.4; see also 45.1.

44. *ST1–2* 103.4.

45. "Sanguis Christi obligat filios Iudaeorum inquantum sunt imitatores paternae malitiae ipsam approbando." *QDM* 4.8 ad 9.

46. *REM* 8.12, 12.43.

47. *CRO* 10.1.

48. "Habere fidem non est in natura humana: sed in natura humana est ut mens hominis non repugnet interiori instinctui et exteriori veritatis praedicationi. Unde infidelitas secundum hoc est contra naturam." *ST2–2* 10.1 ad 1.

Chapter 5

1. "Potest etiam designare terminum, quia videlicet usque tunc caecitas Iudaeorum durabit, quousque plenitudo Gentium ad fidem intrabit. Et huic concordat quod intra subdit de futuro remedio Iudaeorum, cum dicit et tunc, scilicet cum plenitudo Gentium intraverit, omnis Israel salvus fiet, non particulariter sicut modo, sed universaliter omnes." *CRO* 11.4.

2. "Propter suam impoenitentiam sunt in omnes Gentes dispersi. Et sic Christus et Ecclesia ubique a libris Iudaeorum testimonium habuit fidei christianae, ad convertendos Gentiles qui suspicari potuissent prophetias de Christo, quas praedicatores fidei inducebant, esse confictas, nisi probarentur testimonio Iudaeorum." *CRO* 11.2. Earlier in the same commentary Thomas refers to the Jews as "our lackeys," servile guardians of the Hebrew scriptures that give proof to the Christian faith. "Iudaei sunt nostri capsarii, custodientes libros ex quibus nostrae fidei testimonium perhibetur." *CRO* 9.2.

3. Aquinas's social teaching has received more attention than other aspects of his thought on the Jews; still, considering the scope of Thomistic scholarship, the relevant literature is slight. J. Guttman, *Das Verhaltniss des Thomas von Aquino zum Judenthum und zur judischen Litteratur* (Gottingen: Vandenhoeck and Ruprecht's, 1891), 1–15, summarizes the main points of Aquinas's teaching, but his real focus is the philosophic influence on Aquinas of Jewish thinkers such as Maimonides and Al Gazali. A. Broadie, "Medieval Jewry Through the Eyes of Aquinas" is little more than an apologetic paraphrase of *ST2–2* 10.7–12. Gilbert Dahan, *Les intellectuels chretiens et les juifs au moyen age* (Paris: Editions du Cerf, 1990), frequently refers to Aquinas's views in the context of a broader survey. H. Liebeschutz, "Judaism and Jewry in the Social Doctrine of Thomas Aquinas," *Journal of Jewish Studies* 12 (1962): 57–81, and Bernhard Blumenkranz, "Le *De regime Iudaeorum*: ses modeles, son exemple," are more helpful. Liebeschutz places Aquinas in the context of thirteenth-century economic and political developments, and also compares his teaching with other scholastics. On the whole he finds Aquinas rather tolerant and regards the subsequent fate of European Jews as evidence that his teaching had

little influence. Blumenkranz disagrees on both counts: he finds Aquinas less tolerant than contemporary popes, for example, and argues that those who persecuted Jews "pouvait se nourrir a la source du docteur angelique." The articles by Broadie and Blumenkranz are conveniently collected in *Aquinas and Problems of His Time*, G. Verbeke and D. Verhelst (Louvain: Louvain University Press, 1976), 57–68 and 101–17.

4. *ChJ*, 13.

5. "Turbato corde audivimus, et narramus, quod non solum quidam de Judaicae coecitatis errore ad lumen Fidei Christianae conversi ad priorem reversi esse perfidiam dignoscuntur; verum etiam quamplurimi Christiani veritatem Catholicae Fidei abnegantes se damnabiliter ad ritum Judaicum transtulerunt; Quod tanto magis reprobum fore cognoscitur, quanto ex hoc Christi Nomen Sanctissimum quadam familiari hostilitate securius blasphematur." From *Turbato Corde*, a letter sent on 1 March 1274 by Pope Gregory X to "the friars of the Dominican and Franciscan Orders who are or will be deputized by the Holy See as inquisitors of heresy." *ChJ* 2, 33. This letter, like a similar one issued in 1267 by Clement IV (*ChJ* 2, 26), was instrumental in giving the Inquisition the authority to interrogate Jews.

6. Edward Synan, *The Popes and the Jews in the Middle Ages* (New York: Seton Hall, 1965), 155. For an opposing view, see Edouard Will and Claude Orrieux, *Proselytisme juif?* (Paris: Belles Lettres, 1992).

7. *REM* 23.15.

8. See above, 24–25.

9. On the drive for system and uniformity and for an analysis of the increasing burdens placed on European Jews in the context of efforts to marginalize other groups such as heretics, lepers, and homosexuals, see R. I. Moore, *The Formation of a Persecuting Society: 1100–1250* (Oxford: Basil Blackwell, 1987). In a similar vein, James A. Brundage, *Law, Sex, and Christian Society in Medieval Europe* (Chicago: University of Chicago Press, 1987), analyzes efforts to develop and enforce laws governing sexual behavior during this period.

10. Hyam Maccoby, *Judaism on Trial* (Rutherford, N.J.: Fairleigh Dickinson University Press, 1982), 121.

11. "Melius dicendum quod refertur ad pacem factam per Christum, que complebitur in futuro." *CIS* 2.4.

12. See E. I. J. Rosenthal, "Anti-Christian Polemic in Medieval Bible Commentaries," *Journal of Jewish Studies* 3–4 (1960): 115–35.

13. *SBMA*, 164.

14. *ST1* 1.10 ad 1; *QDL* 7.14–16.

15. For a summary of these arguments, see Daniel J. Lasker, *Jewish Philosophical Polemics Against Christianity in the Middle Ages* (New York: Ktav, 1977).

16. Maimonides rejection of "positive attributes" in God may have been based in part on this consideration; *Guide* 1.58. Aquinas was aware of his arguments and responded to them: *ST1* 13.2.

17. Lasker, *Jewish Polemics*, 105.

18. Lasker, *Jewish Polemics*, 135–51.

19. This section of the *Summa* was written in late 1271 or early 1272. Thus almost all of the most important texts for his thought on the Jews—the commen-

taries on John, Romans, and Psalms, the *Summa*, and the letter entitled *De Regimine Iudaeorum*—were written between 1268 and 1274.

20. *ST2–2 Prologus.*

21. Aquinas was more interested in the sources of human action than in moral principles or rules; hence he organized his treatise on morality according to moral habits or dispositions—virtues and vices—rather than following the order of the Ten Commandments. Since Kant, however, moral philosophy has largely focused on moral principles and casuistry. Thomists have had similar interests; witness the mass of secondary literature on Aquinas's theory of natural law and the relative neglect of his treatment of moral habits.

22. Aquinas did not himself provide titles for the articles in the *Summa*; this was done by his disciples after his death. On occasion these titles can be misleading, but in the case of *ST2–2* 10 they accurately reflect the queries that begin each article.

23. "In illis qui nihil audierunt de fide, [infidelitas] non habet rationem peccati, sed magis poenae, quia talis ignorantia divinorum ex peccato primi parentis est consecuta. Qui autem sic sunt infideles damnantur quidem propter alia peccata, quae sine fide remitti non possunt; non autem damnantur propter infidelitatis peccatum." *ST2–2* 10.1.

24. "Quia suscepereunt eius figuram in veteri lege . . . ipsorum infidelitas est gravius peccatum quam infidelitas gentilium, qui nullo modo fidem Evangelii susceperunt." *ST2–2* 10.6.

25. *ST2–2* 10.8, corpus and ad 2 and ad 4.

26. "In nullo modo sunt ad fidem compellendi, ut ipsi credant." *ST2–2* 10.8.

27. *ST2–2* 10.8 obj. 2. The passage quoted is from the canon *De Iudaeis*, D. 45, c. 5.

28. "Susceperunt eius figuram in veteri lege." *ST2–2* 10.6.

29. Liebeschutz, "Social Doctrine", 163. Broadie, "Medieval Jewry," 57, claims that Aquinas's social teaching on Jews is part of a unified world-view which does follow from his theological ideas about Judaism. But this is merely an assertion; he makes no effort to demonstrate his thesis.

30. "Qui fuissent inviti et reluctantes immersi, saltem ratione sacramenti ad jurisdictionem ecclesiasticam pertinerent; unde ad servandam regulam fidei Christiane forent rationabiliter compellendi. Verum id est religioni christiane contrarium, ut semper invitus et penitus contradicens ad recipiendam et servandam Christianitatem aliquis compellatur. Propter quod inter invitum et invitum, coactum et coactum, alii non absurde distinguunt, quod is qui terroribus atque suppliciis violenter attrahitur, et ne detrimentum incurrat. Baptismi suscipit sacramentum . . . [et] characterem suscipit Christianitatis impressum, et ipse tanquam conditionaliter volens, licet absolute non velit, cogendus est ad observantiam fidei Christiane . . . ne nomen Domini blasphemetur, et fides quam susceperunt vilis ac contemptibilis habeatur. Ille vero qui numquam consentit, sed penitus contradicit, nec rem nec characterem suscipit sacramenti, quia plus est expresse contradicere quam minime consentire . . ." *X* 3.42.3; *ChJ* n. 12.

31. *ST1–2* 6.6.

32. The incestuous relationship among *ST2–2* 10.12, *ST3* 68.10, and *QDL* 2.4.2 raises a number of interesting questions that have implications both for the role

played by editors in putting together the *Summa Theologiae* and for the relation of the text of "quodlibetal" or occasional questions and the public university debates they supposedly record. *ST2–2* 10.12, which Thomas wrote in late 1271 or early 1272, is in fact a doublet of the quodlibet, which was disputed at Paris in late 1269, while *ST3* 68.10 (a condensed version of *QDL* 2.4.2/*ST2–2* 10.12), was written sometime in the months before 6 December 1273, when Thomas had his famous breakdown and stopped work on the *Summa* at *ST3* 90.4. Thus we have the scenario of Thomas inserting, without alteration, a quodlibetal question into the *Summa*, then, a year and a half later, revisiting the same question, re-editing his own text, and inserting it yet again. Intuitively, something seems amiss here; I suspect a later editor may have had a hand in *ST3* 68.10. In any case, the fact that the text of a quodlibetal question, which supposedly reflects a genuine university debate, can be fitted so seamlessly into the *Summa* makes one wonder what, if anything, such texts can tell us about the actual course of such debates.

33. It is notable as well that while the query that begins the article asks whether the children of Jews "or other unbelievers" should be baptized against their parents' wishes, in the corpus of the article Aquinas refers specifically—and exclusively—to Jewish children.

34. "Filius enim naturaliter est aliquid patris. Et primo quidem a parentibus non distinguitur secundum corpus, quandiu in matris utero continetur. Postmodum vero, postquam ab utero egreditur, antequam usum liberi arbitrii habeat, continetur sub parentum cura sicut sub quodam spirituali utero . . . ita de iure naturali est quod filius, antequam habeat usum rationis, sit sub cura patris. Unde contra iustitiam naturalem esset si puer, antequam habeat usum rationis, a cura parentum subtrahatur, vel de eo aliquid ordinetur invitis parentibus." *ST2–2* 10.12. The final phrase, "de eo aliquid ordinetur invitis parentibus" is difficult to render in English. *Ordinare* literally means to order or direct, but in Aquinas it often means—as it does here—to orient one's entire being toward a final end. The term also has specifically religious connotations: to consecrate a priest or bishop is to *ordinare*, and to be a monk, nun, or friar is to be a member of an *ordo*. Thus to baptize a child involves determining its most basic spiritual direction as well as imposing spiritual obligations on it.

35. These objections are repeated in *ST3* 68.10, whereas the other two are omitted.

36. Dieter Berg examines Aquinas's views on the doctrine of Jewish servitude in "*Servitus Iudaeorum*: Zum Verhaltnis des Thomas von Aquin und seines Ordens zu den Juden in Europa im 13. Jahrhundert," in *Thomas von Aquin: Werk und Wirkung im Licht neuerer Forschungen*, ed. A Zimmermann (Berlin, 1988). I agree with his conclusion that the doctrine had little direct influence on Aquinas's social teaching.

37. "Quilibet homo magis est Dei, a quo habet animam, quam patris carnalis, a quo habet corpus. Non ergo est iniustum si pueri Iudaeorum carnalibus parentibus auferantur et Deo per baptismum consecrentur." *ST2–2* 10.12 obj. 4. Note that here the objection specifically proposes not just baptizing the children, but also taking them from their parents.

38. "Homo ordinatur ad Deum per rationem, per quam eum cognoscere

potest. Unde puer, antequam usum rationis habeat, naturali ordine ordinatur in Deum per rationem parentum, quorum curae naturaliter subiacet; et secundum ipsum divina agenda." *ST1–2* 10.12 ad 4.

39. Scotus dismissed Thomas's argument in a single sentence: "In parvulo Deus habet maius ius dominii quam parentes." *Opera Omnia* vol. 16 (Paris: L. Vives, 1895), 487.

40. "Iudaei ritus suos observant, in quibus olim praefigurabatur veritas fidei quam tenemus, hoc bonum provenit quod testimonium fidei nostrae habemus ab hostibus, et quasi in figura nobis repraesentatur quod credimus. Et ideo in suis ritibus tolerantur." *ST2–2* 10.11. Aquinas goes on to add that pagans and heretics should be allowed to worship only if a ban would harm Christian missionary efforts or in other ways undermine the interests of the Church; normally, however, such worship should be suppressed.

41. *RPS* 39.4.

42. "Scandalum quoque per eos in Ecclesia Christi non modicum generatur, quod cum ipsi carnibus animalium, que mectant fideles, vesci abhorreant ut immundis, istud obtinent principum ex favore quod mactanda carnifices animalia tradunt illis, qui ea ritu Iudaico laniantes, ex ipsis accipiunt quantum volunt, relicto residuo Christianis. . . . Aliud quoque presumunt non minus istis detestabile Christianis, quod vindemiarum tempore uvas calcat Iudeus lineis caligis calceatus, et puriori eodem, residuum, quasi foedatum ab ipsis, reliquentes fidelibus Christianis; ex quo interdum sanguinis Christi conficitur sacramentum." *ChJ*, 24.

43. Exceptions to this rule could arise when ecclesiastical officials are also secular rulers. Thus Aquinas claimed it was legitimate for such rulers to forbid Jews and pagans to associate with Christians as a punishment for certain crimes ("propter aliquas speciales culpas"): *ST2–2* 10.9 ad 2.

44. "Videtur esse distinguendum secundum diversas conditiones personarum et negotiorum et temporum. Si enim aliqui fuerint firmi in fide, ita quod ex communione eorum cum infidelibus conversio infidelium magis sperari possit quam fidelium a fide aversio; non sunt prohibendi infidelibus communicare qui fidem non susceperunt, scilicet paganis vel Iudaeis, et maxime si necessitas urgeat. Si autem sint simplices et infirmi in fide, de quorum subversione probabiliter timeri possit, prohibendi sunt ab infidelium communione: et praecipue ne magnam familiaritatem cum eis habeant, vel absque necessitate eis communicent." *ST2–2* 10.9.

45. Cases of pagan or Jewish slaves converting to Christianity presented a more complicated case. In lands held by the Church "vel eius membris," slaves owned by Jews who accepted Christianity were to be freed, with no compensation paid to their owners. This was not unjust, Aquinas argued; since Jews are slaves of the Church, "potest disponere de rebus eorum." If the slaves had been purchased specifically for resale, however, their owners were given three months to sell them to Christian owners. The latter provision was to avoid any appearance of injustice. *ST2–2* 10.10.

46. Maccoby, 147.

47. "Non debet disputari de his quae sunt fidei quasi de eis dubitando: sed propter veritatem manifestandam et errores confutandos." *ST2–2* 10.7 ad 3.

48. "Quorum fides ex hoc est firmior quod nihil diversum audierunt ab eo quod credunt." *ST2–2* 10.7.

49. "Dicit 'qui eripiat,' propter paucos, qui nunc difficulter quasi cum quadam violentia convertuntur. . . . Dicit autem 'avertet impietatem a Iacob,' ad ostendendum facilitatem conversionis Iudaeorum in fine mundi." *CRO* 11.4.

50. AH,*ST* Inq. III, Tract. VIII, Sect. I, Q. I, Tit. II, M. 1, c. 1. The response is simply that Jewish books containing blasphemy should be burnt, and any Jew who persistently and publicly blasphemes should be appropriately punished: "Libri eorum, in quibus huiusmodi blasphemiae continentur, comburendi sunt; ipsi vero, si pertinaciter in huiusmodi blasphemia persisterent, coram iudice convicti, digna poena sunt puniendi. Secus autem est, si occulte blasphemant."

51. AH,*ST* Inq. II, Tract VII, Sect. L, Q. I, Tit. II, M. 1, c.5 and M. 2 c. 3.

52. AH,*ST* Inq. III, Tract. VIII, Sect. I, Q. L, Tit. II, M. I, c. 4.

53. Blumenkranz, "Le *De Regimine Iudaeorum*," 101.

54. Ibid., 101.

55. "Quia mihi placeret ut super hiis requireretis consilium aliorum magis in talibus peritorum." *DRI* 12–14.

56. "Si liceat vobis aliquo tempore et quo exactionem facere in Iudeos." *DRI* 19–21.

57. Aquinas replies along these lines to Marquerite's sixth query: Was it licit to exact tribute from her Christian subjects?

58. "Ad quem quaestionem sic absolute propositam responderi potest, quia licet, ut iura dicunt, Iudaei merito culpae suae sint, vel essent perpetuae servitute addicti, et sic eorum res terrarum domini possint accipere tamquam suas: hoc tamen servato moderaminie, ut necessaria vitae subsidia eis nullatenus subtrahantur." *DRI* 22–28. The *iura* Thomas was referring to, as the Leonine editors note, probably included *Etsi Iudaeos*, *X* 5.6.13: "Etsi Iudeos, quos propria culpa submisit perpetue servituti, cum Dominum crucifixerint . . ." The doctrine of Jewish servitude, of course, was a commonplace of medieval canon law.

59. Thomas here uses the technical legal term "eo qui foris sunt," derived from I Corinthians 5.13, to refer to those who have never accepted the Gospel.

60. "Tamen oportet nos honeste ambulare etiam ad eos qui foris sunt ne nomen Domini blasphemetur, et Apostolus monet fideles suo exemplo ut sine offensione sint Iudeis et Gentibus et Ecclesie Dei, hoc servandum videtur ut, sicut iura determinant, ab eis coacta servitia non exigantur que ipsi preterito tempore facere non consueuerunt, quia ea que sunt insolita magis solent animos perturbare." *DRI* 28–36. Here again Thomas follows the *Decretales* in formulating his reply; he mentions *iura*, and his language closely parallels that of *X* 5.6.9: "Neque aliquis ab eis coacta servitia exigat, nisi ea, quae ipsi tempore praeterito facere consueverunt."

61. "Ad quod plana est responsio, quod, secundum statutum Concilii generalis, Iudei utriusque sexus in omni Christianorum provincia et omni tempore aliquo habitu ab aliis populis debent distingui. Hoc etiam eis in lege eorum mandatur, ut scilicet faciant sibi fimbrias per angulos palliorum, per quas ab aliis discernantur." *DRI* 244–51. Compare the language of the canon: "Statuimus, ut tales utriusque sexus in omni Christianorum provincia, et omni tempore qualitate habitus publice

ab aliis populis distinguantur cum et per Moysen hoc ipsum eis legatur iniunctum." *X* 5.19.5; *ChJ* n. 10.

62. "Accipere usuram pro pecunia mutuata est secundum se iniustum." *ST2–2* 78.1.

63. *ST2–2* 78.1 ad 3.

64. "Quod autem de Iudeis dictum est, idem intelligi debet de Cahorsinis vel quibuscumque aliis insistentibus usurarie pravitati." *DRI* 118–20. Cahors was a notorious center of usury, though in the thirteenth century the term "Cahorsian" was also used to refer to Lombard bankers.

65. "Videtur etiam michi quod esset maiori pena pecuniaria puniendus Iudeus vel quicumque alius usurarius quam aliquis alius in simili casu, quanto pecunia que ei aufertur minus ad eum noscitur pertinere." *DRI* 70–74. Blumenkranz thought this statement implied Jews should be punished more harshly than other usurers: "Innovation encore que la franchise avec laquelle il admet—ce qui était partout pratique courante—que la peine pécuniaire dont pouvait être frappé un Juif condamné devait être plus forte que celle infligée à quelqu'un d'autre dans le même cas" ("Le *De Regimine Iudaeorum*," 109). It is true that *vel* can be used as an intensifying adverb, but it seems clear that here it performs its more common role as the conjunction "or," especially since in the sentence the comparative is "maiori . . . quam." Blumenkranz's reading would be justified only if the phrase "vel quicumque alius usurarius" were omitted altogether.

66. "Si vero dicatur, quod ex hoc principes terrarum dampnificantur, hoc dampnum sibi imputent utpote ex negligentia eorum proveniens: melius enim esset ut Iudeos laborare compellerent ad proprium victum lucrandum, sicut in partibus Ytalie faciunt, quam quod otiosi viventes de solis usuris ditentur et sic eorum domini suis redditibus defraudentur." *DRI* 81–88.

Chapter 6

1. On Aquinas's belief in the ability of custom to acquire force of law, see *ST1–2* 97.3.

2. *FTD*, 486.

3. Blumenkranz, "Le *De Regimine*," 112.

4. Ibid., 112.

Bibliography

Alexandri de Hales. *Summa Theologica*. 4 Vols. Quaracchi: Collegium S. Bonaventurae, 1948.

Augustine. *The City of God*. Translated by Marcus Dods. New York: Random House, 1950.

———. *Tractatus contra Iudaeos*. *PL* 42, 51–63.

Bachrach, Bernard. *Early Medieval Jewish Policy in Western Europe*. Minneapolis: University of Minnesota Press, 1977.

Baer, Yitzhak. "The Disputations of R. Yechiel of Paris and Nachmanides." *Tarbiz* 2 (1931): 185–87.

Baron, Salo W. *A Social and Religious History of the Jews*. 2nd ed. 18 vols. New York: Columbia University Press, 1952–83.

Berg, Dieter. "*Servitus Iudaeorum*. Zum Verhaltnis des Thomas von Aquin und seines Ordens zu den Juden in Europa im 13. Jahrhundert." In *Thomas von Aquin: Werk und Wirkungim Licht neuerer Forschungen*, edited by Albert Zimmermann. Berlin, 1988.

Berger, David. "Mission to the Jews and Jewish-Christians Contacts in the Polemical Literature of the High Middle Ages." *American Historical Review* 91 (1986): 576–91.

Blumenkranz, Bernhard. "Augustin et les juifs; Augustin et le judaisme." *Recherches Augustiniennes* 1 (1958): 225–41.

———. *Les auteurs chrétiens latins du moyen âge sur les juifs et le judaisme, 430–1096*. Paris: Mouton, 1963.

———. "Le *De Regimine Iudaeorum*: ses modéles, son exemple." In *Aquinas and Problems of His Time*, edited by G. Verbeke and D. Verhelst, 101–17. Louvain: Louvain University Press, 1976.

———. *Die Judenpredigt Augustins*. Basel: Helbing and Lichtenhahn, 1946.

———. *Juifs et chrétiens dans le monde occidental*. Paris: Mouton, 1960.

———. *Le juif medieval au miroir de l'art chrétien*. Paris: Mouton, 1966.

Broadie, Alexander. "Medieval Jewry through the Eyes of Aquinas." In *Aquinas and Problems of His Time*, edited by G. Verbeke and D. Verhelst, 57–69. Louvain: Louvain University Press, 1976.

Brundage, James. *Law, Sex, and Christian Society in Medieval Europe*. Chicago: University of Chicago Press, 1987.

Chavel, Charles B. *Kitvei Rabbenu Mosheh ben Nahman*, Vol. 1. Jerusalem, 1963.

Chazan, Robert. *Barcelona and Beyond*. Berkeley: University of California Press, 1992.

———. "The Barcelona 'Disputation' of 1263: Christian Missionizing and Jewish Response." *Speculum* 52 (1977): 824–42.

———. *Daggers of Faith*. Berkeley: University of California Press, 1989.
———. *Medieval Jewry in Northern France: A Political and Social History*. Baltimore and London: Johns Hopkins University Press, 1973.
Cohen, Jeremy. *The Friars and the Jews*. Ithaca: Cornell University Press, 1982.
———. "The Jews as the Killers of Christ in the Latin Tradition from Augustine to the Friars." *Traditio* 39 (1983): 1–27.
Cohen, Martin A. "Reflections on the Text and Context of the Disputation of Barcelona." *Hebrew Union College Annual* 35 (1964): 157–92.
Corpus iuris canonici. Ed. Aemilius Friedburg. Leipzig, 1879–81. Repr. Graz, 1959.
Dahan, Gilbert. *Les intellectuels chrétiens et les juifs au moyen age*. Paris: Editions du Cerf, 1990.
———. "Saint Bonaventure et les juifs." *Archivum Franciscanum Historicum* 77 (1984): 369–405.
Deploige, S. *S. Thomas et la question juive*. Louvain, 1897.
Duns Scotus. *Opera Omnia*. Paris: L. Vives, 1891–95.
Flannery, Austin, ed. *Vatican Council II: The Conciliar and Post Conc] iliar Documents*. Northport, N.Y.: Costello, 1975.
Gager, John. *The Origins of Anti-Semitism*. London: Oxford University Press, 1985.
Gaston, Lloyd. "Paul and the Torah." In *Antisemitism and the Foundations of Christianity*, edited by Alan Davies, 48–71. New York: Paulist Press, 1979.
Gayraud, H. *L'antisemitisme de S. Thomas d'Aquin*. Paris, 1896.
Grayzel, Solomon. *The Church and the Jews in the Thirteenth Century, 1198–1254*. Philadelphia: Dropsie University Press, 1933.
———. "The Jews and Roman Law." *Jewish Quarterly Review* 59 (1968): 93–117.
———. "The Papal Bull *Sicut Iudaeis*." In *Studies and Essays in Honor of Abraham A. Neuman*, edited by Meir Ben-Horin et al, 243–80. Philadelphia: Dropsie University Press, 1962.
———. "Popes, Jews, and Inquisition from 'Sicut' to 'Turbato.'" In *Essays on the Occasion of the Seventieth Anniversary of Dropsie University*, edited by A.L. Katsch et al., 151–88. Philadelphia: Dropsie University Press, 1979.
———. "The Talmud and the Medieval Papacy." In *Essays in Honor of Solomon B. Freehof*, edited by Walter Jacob et al., 220–45. Pittsburg: Rodef Shalom Congregation, 1964.
Grayzel, Solomon, and Stow, Kenneth. *The Church and the Jews in the Thirteenth Century, 1254–1314*. Vol. 2. New York and Detroit: Wayne State University Press, 1989.
Grisez, Germain. "The First Principle of Practical Reason: A Commentary on *Summa Theologiae* 1–2, Question 94, Article 2." In *Aquinas: A Collection of Critical Essays*, edited by Anthony Kenny, 340–82. Garden City [N.Y.]: Anchor Books, 1969.
Guttman, J. *Das Verhaltniss des Thomas von Aquino zum Judenthum und zur judischen Litteratur*. Gottingen: Vandenhoeck and Ruprecht's, 1891.
Harkins, Paul, ed. *Discourses Against Judaizing Christians*. Washington, D.C.: Catholic University Press, 1979.
Huizinga, J. *The Waning of the Middle Ages*. New York, Doubleday, 1954.
Jordan, William C. *The French Monarchy and the Jews*. Philadelphia: University of Pennsylvania Press, 1989.

Katz, Jacob. *Exclusiveness and Tolerance*. London: Oxford University Press, 1963.

Katz, S. "Gregory the Great and the Jews." *Jewish Quarterly Review* 24 (1933–34): 113–36.

Langmuir, Gavin. *History, Religion, and Antisemitism*. Berkeley: University of California Press, 1990.

———. *Toward a Definition of Antisemitism*. Berkeley: University of California Press, 1990.

Lasker, Daniel J. *Jewish Philosophical Polemics Against Christianity in the Middle Ages*. New York: Ktav, 1977.

Liebeschutz, Hans. "Judaism and Jewry in the Social Doctrine of Thomas Aquinas." *Journal of Jewish Studies* 12 (1961): 57–81.

Little, Lester. *Religious Poverty and the Profit Economy in Medieval Europe*. Ithaca, N.Y.: Cornell University Press, 1978.

Maccoby, Hyam. *Judaism on Trial*. Rutherford, N.J.: Fairleigh Dickinson University Press, 1982.

Mailloux, B. *S. Thomas et les juifs*. Montreal, 1935.

Mansi, Giovanni Domenico, ed. *Sacrorum conciliorum nova et amplissima Collectio*. 60 vols. Paris: Hubert Welter, 1901–27.

Moore, R. I. *The Formation of a Persecuting Society: 1100–1250*. New York and Oxford: Basil Blackwell, 1987.

Moses Maimonides. *The Guide of the Perplexed*. Translated by Shlomo Pines. Chicago: University of Chicago Press, 1963.

Patrologia cursus completus . . . series Latina. Ed. J.-P. Migne. 221 vols. Paris: J.-P. Migne, 1844–64.

Peter Lombard. *Sententiae in IV Libris Distinctae*. Grottaferrata: Collegium S. Bonaventurae, 1971–81.

Reuther, Rosemary. *Faith and Fratricide*. New York: Seabury Press, 1974.

Rosenthal, E. I. J. "Anti-Christian Polemic in Medieval Bible Commentaries." *Journal of Jewish Studies* 3–4 (1960): 115–35.

Roth, C. "The Disputation of Barcelona." *Harvard Theological Review* 43 (1950): 117–44.

Schooner, H. V. "La *Lectura super Matthaeum* V, 20–48 de Thomas d'Aquin." *Recherches de theologie ancienne et medievale* 50 (1983): 145–90.

Silver, Daniel J. *Maimonidean Criticism and the Maimonidean Controversy, 1180–1240*. Leiden: E.J. Brill, 1965.

Simon, Marcel. *Verus Israel*. Translated by H. McKeating. London: Oxford University Press, 1986.

Simonsohn, Shlomo. *The Apostolic See and the Jews: Documents, 492–1404*. Toronto: Pontifical Institute for Medieval Studies, 1988.

Smalley, Beryl. *The Study of the Bible in the Middle Ages*. 3rd edition. London: Oxford University Press, 1983.

———. "William of Auvergne, John of La Rochelle, and Thomas Aquinas on the Old Law." In *St. Thomas Aquinas Commemorative Studies*, edited by Amand Maurer et al., 11–71. Toronto: Pontifical Institute for Medieval Studies, 1974.

Southern, R. W. *The Making of the Middle Ages*. New Haven, Conn. and London: Yale University Press, 1953.

———. *Western Society and the Church in the Middle Ages*. New York: Penguin, 1970.

Stow, Kenneth R. *Alienated Minority: The Jews of Medieval Latin Europe*. Cambridge, Mass.: Harvard University Press, 1992.

———. *The "1007 Anonymous" and Papal Sovereignty*. Cincinnati: Hebrew Union College and The Jewish Institute of Religion, 1984.

Synan, E. *The Popes and the Jews in the Middle Ages*. New York: Seton Hall, 1965.

Thomas Aquinas. *Opera Omnia*. Ed. Roberto Busa. 7 vols. Holzboog: Friedrich Fromann, 1980.

Weisheipl, James A. *Friar Thomas D'Aquino*. Washington, D.C.: Catholic University Press, 1974.

Wilken, Robert L. *John Chrysostom and the Jews*. Berkeley: University of California Press, 1983.

Will, Edouard, and Claude Orrieux. *Proselytisme juif?* Paris: Belles Lettres, 1992.

Williams, A. Lukyn. *Adversus Judaeos*. Cambridge: Cambridge University Press, 1935.

Zuckerman, A. J. "The Political Uses of Theology: The Conflict of Bishop Agobard and the Jews of Lyons." *Studies in Medieval Culture* 3 (1970): 23–51.

Index

University of Pennsylvania Press
MIDDLE AGES SERIES
Edward Peters, General Editor

F. R. P. Akehurst, trans. *The* Coutumes de Beauvaisis *of Philippe de Beaumanoir*. 1992

Peter L. Allen. *The Art of Love: Amatory Fiction from Ovid to the* Romance of the Rose. 1992

David Anderson. *Before the Knight's Tale: Imitation of Classical Epic in Boccaccio's* Teseida. 1988

Benjamin Arnold. *Count and Bishop in Medieval Germany: A Study of Regional Power, 1100–1350*. 1991

Mark C. Bartusis. *The Late Byzantine Army: Arms and Society, 1204–1453*. 1992

Thomas N. Bisson, ed. *Cultures of Power: Lordship, Status, and Process in Twelfth-Century Europe*. 1995

Uta-Renate Blumenthal. *The Investiture Controversy: Church and Monarchy from the Ninth to the Twelfth Century*. 1988

Gerald A. Bond. *The Loving Subject: Desire, Eloquence, and Power in Romanesque France*. 1995

Daniel Bornstein, trans. *Dino Compagni's* Chronicle *of Florence*. 1986

Maureen Boulton. *The Song in the Story: Lyric Insertions in French Narrative Fiction, 1200–1400*. 1993

Betsy Bowden. *Chaucer Aloud: The Varieties of Textual Interpretation*. 1987

Charles R. Bowlus. *Franks, Moravians, and Magyars: The Struggle for the Middle Danube, 788–907*. 1995

James William Brodman. *Ransoming Captives in Crusader Spain: The Order of Merced on the Christian-Islamic Frontier*. 1986

Kevin Brownlee and Sylvia Huot, eds. *Rethinking the* Romance of the Rose*: Text, Image, Reception*. 1992

Matilda Tomaryn Bruckner. *Shaping Romance: Interpretation, Truth, and Closure in Twelfth-Century French Fictions*. 1993

Otto Brunner (Howard Kaminsky and James Van Horn Melton, eds. and trans.). Land *and Lordship: Structures of Governance in Medieval Austria*. 1992

Robert I. Burns, S.J., ed. *Emperor of Culture: Alfonso X the Learned of Castile and His Thirteenth-Century Renaissance*. 1990

David Burr. *Olivi and Franciscan Poverty: The Origins of the* Usus Pauper *Controversy*. 1989

David Burr. *Olivi's Peaceable Kingdom: A Reading of the Apocalypse Commentary*. 1993

Thomas Cable. *The English Alliterative Tradition*. 1991

Anthony K. Cassell and Victoria Kirkham, eds. and trans. *Diana's Hunt/Caccia di Diana: Boccaccio's First Fiction*. 1991

John C. Cavadini. *The Last Christology of the West: Adoptionism in Spain and Gaul, 785–820*. 1993

Brigitte Cazelles. *The Lady as Saint: A Collection of French Hagiographic Romances of the Thirteenth Century*. 1991

Karen Cherewatuk and Ulrike Wiethaus, eds. *Dear Sister: Medieval Women and the Epistolary Genre*. 1993

Anne L. Clark. *Elisabeth of Schönau: A Twelfth-Century Visionary*. 1992

Willene B. Clark and Meradith T. McMunn, eds. *Beasts and Birds of the Middle Ages: The Bestiary and Its Legacy*. 1989

Richard C. Dales. *The Scientific Achievement of the Middle Ages*. 1973

Charles T. Davis. *Dante's Italy and Other Essays*. 1984

William J. Dohar. *The Black Death and Pastoral Leadership: The Diocese of Hereford in the Fourteenth Century*. 1994

Katherine Fischer Drew, trans. *The Burgundian Code*. 1972

Katherine Fischer Drew, trans. *The Laws of the Salian Franks*. 1991

Katherine Fischer Drew, trans. *The Lombard Laws*. 1973

Nancy Edwards. *The Archaeology of Early Medieval Ireland*. 1990

Richard K. Emmerson and Ronald B. Herzman. *The Apocalyptic Imagination in Medieval Literature*. 1992

Theodore Evergates. *Feudal Society in Medieval France: Documents from the County of Champagne*. 1993

Felipe Fernández-Armesto. *Before Columbus: Exploration and Colonization from the Mediterranean to the Atlantic, 1229–1492*. 1987

Jerold C. Frakes. *Brides and Doom: Gender, Property, and Power in Medieval Women's Epic*. 1994

R. D. Fulk. *A History of Old English Meter*. 1992

Patrick J. Geary. *Aristocracy in Provence: The Rhône Basin at the Dawn of the Carolingian Age*. 1985

Peter Heath. *Allegory and Philosophy in Avicenna (Ibn Sînâ), with a Translation of the Book of the Prophet Muḥammad's Ascent to Heaven*. 1992

J. N. Hillgarth, ed. *Christianity and Paganism, 350–750: The Conversion of Western Europe*. 1986

Richard C. Hoffmann. *Land, Liberties, and Lordship in a Late Medieval Countryside: Agrarian Structures and Change in the Duchy of Wrocław*. 1990

Robert Hollander. *Boccaccio's Last Fiction: Il Corbaccio*. 1988

John Y. B. Hood. *Aquinas and the Jews*. 1995

Edward B. Irving, Jr. *Rereading* Beowulf. 1989

Richard A. Jackson, ed. Ordines Coronationis Franciae*: Texts and Ordines for the Coronation of Frankish and French Kings and Queens in the Middle Ages, Vol. I*. 1995

C. Stephen Jaeger. *The Envy of Angels: Cathedral Schools and Social Ideals in Medieval Europe, 950–1200*. 1994

C. Stephen Jaeger. *The Origins of Courtliness: Civilizing Trends and the Formation of Courtly Ideals, 939–1210*. 1985

Donald J. Kagay, trans. *The Usatges of Barcelona: The Fundamental Law of Catalonia*. 1994

Richard Kay. *Dante's Christian Astrology*. 1994
Ellen E. Kittell. *From* Ad Hoc *to Routine: A Case Study in Medieval Bureaucracy*. 1991
Alan C. Kors and Edward Peters, eds. *Witchcraft in Europe, 1100-1700: A Documentary History*. 1972
Barbara M. Kreutz. *Before the Normans: Southern Italy in the Ninth and Tenth Centuries*. 1992
Michael P. Kuczynski. *Prophetic Song: The Psalms as Moral Discourse in Late Medieval England*. 1995
E. Ann Matter. *The Voice of My Beloved: The Song of Songs in Western Medieval Christianity*. 1990
Shannon McSheffrey. *Gender and Heresy: Women and Men in Lollard Communities, 1420–1530*. 1995
A. J. Minnis. *Medieval Theory of Authorship*. 1988
Lawrence Nees. *A Tainted Mantle: Hercules and the Classical Tradition at the Carolingian Court*. 1991
Lynn H. Nelson, trans. *The Chronicle of San Juan de la Peña: A Fourteenth-Century Official History of the Crown of Aragon*. 1991
Barbara Newman. *From Virile Woman to WomanChrist: Studies in Medieval Religion and Literature*. 1995
Joseph F. O'Callaghan. *The Learned King: The Reign of Alfonso X of Castile*. 1993
Odo of Tournai (Irven M. Resnick, trans.). *Two Theological Treatises:* On Original Sin *and* A Disputation with the Jew, Leo, Concerning the Advent of Christ, the Son of God. 1994
David M. Olster. *Roman Defeat, Christian Response, and the Literary Construction of the Jew*. 1994
William D. Paden, ed. *The Voice of the Trobairitz: Perspectives on the Women Troubadours*. 1989
Edward Peters. *The Magician, the Witch, and the Law*. 1982
Edward Peters, ed. *Christian Society and the Crusades, 1198–1229: Sources in Translation, including* The Capture of Damietta *by Oliver of Paderborn*. 1971
Edward Peters, ed. *The First Crusade: The* Chronicle of Fulcher of Chartres *and Other Source Materials*. 1971
Edward Peters, ed. *Heresy and Authority in Medieval Europe*. 1980
James M. Powell. *Albertanus of Brescia: The Pursuit of Happiness in the Early Thirteenth Century*. 1992
James M. Powell. *Anatomy of a Crusade, 1213–1221*. 1986
Susan A. Rabe. *Faith, Art, and Politics at Saint-Riquier: The Symbolic Vision of Angilbert*. 1995
Jean Renart (Patricia Terry and Nancy Vine Durling, trans.). *The Romance of the Rose or Guillaume de Dole*. 1993
Michael Resler, trans. Erec *by Hartmann von Aue*. 1987
Pierre Riché (Michael Idomir Allen, trans.). *The Carolingians: A Family Who Forged Europe*. 1993
Pierre Riché (Jo Ann McNamara, trans.). *Daily Life in the World of Charlemagne*. 1978
Jonathan Riley-Smith. *The First Crusade and the Idea of Crusading*. 1986

Joel T. Rosenthal. *Patriarchy and Families of Privilege in Fifteenth-Century England.* 1991

Teofilo F. Ruiz. *Crisis and Continuity: Land and Town in Late Medieval Castile.* 1994

James A. Rushing, Jr. *Images of Adventure: Ywain in the Visual Arts.* 1995

James A. Schultz. *The Knowledge of Childhood in the German Middle Ages, 1100–1350.* 1995

Pamela Sheingorn, ed. and trans. *The Book of Sainte Foy.* 1995

Robin Chapman Stacey. *The Road to Judgment: From Custom to Court in Medieval Ireland and Wales.* 1994

Sarah Stanbury. *Seeing the* Gawain-*Poet: Description and the Act of Perception.* 1992

Robert D. Stevick. *The Earliest Irish and English Bookarts: Visual and Poetic Forms Before A.D. 1000.* 1994

Thomas C. Stillinger. *The Song of Troilus: Lyric Authority in the Medieval Book.* 1992

Susan Mosher Stuard. *A State of Deference: Ragusa/Dubrovnik in the Medieval Centuries.* 1992

Susan Mosher Stuard, ed. *Women in Medieval History and Historiography.* 1987

Susan Mosher Stuard, ed. *Women in Medieval Society.* 1976

Jonathan Sumption. *The Hundred Years War: Trial by Battle.* 1992

Ronald E. Surtz. *The Guitar of God: Gender, Power, and Authority in the Visionary World of Mother Juana de la Cruz (1481–1534).* 1990

Ronald E. Surtz. *Writing Women in Late Medieval and Early Modern Spain: The Mothers of Saint Teresa of Avila.* 1995

Del Sweeney, ed. *Agriculture in the Middle Ages.* 1995

William H. TeBrake. *A Plague of Insurrection: Popular Politics and Peasant Revolt in Flanders, 1323–1328.* 1993

Patricia Terry, trans. *Poems of the Elder Edda.* 1990

Hugh M. Thomas. *Vassals, Heiresses, Crusaders, and Thugs: The Gentry of Angevin Yorkshire, 1154–1216.* 1993

Mary F. Wack. *Lovesickness in the Middle Ages: The* Viaticum *and Its Commentaries.* 1990

Benedicta Ward. *Miracles and the Medieval Mind: Theory, Record, and Event, 1000–1215.* 1982

Suzanne Fonay Wemple. *Women in Frankish Society: Marriage and the Cloister, 500–900.* 1981

Kenneth Baxter Wolf. *Making History: The Normans and Their Historians in Eleventh-Century Italy.* 1995

Jan M. Ziolkowski. *Talking Animals: Medieval Latin Beast Poetry, 750–1150.* 1993

This book has been set in Linotron Galliard. Galliard was designed for Mergenthaler in 1978 by Matthew Carter. Galliard retains many of the features of a sixteenth-century typeface cut by Robert Granjon but has some modifications that give it a more contemporary look.

Printed on acid-free paper.